101

Publishing Tips for Speakers & Consultants

Celia Rocks and Dottie DeHart

ISBN: 0-9748299-0-0

Library of Congress Control Number: 2004101705

Published By:
Pittsburgh Professional Publishing
306 Marberry Drive
Pittsburgh, PA 15215
To order multiple copies of this publication, please call:
412-784-8811

Book Design: Geoffrey Smith and Andra Keller, Rocks-DeHart Public Relations

Contents

Praise

As I write these words, I am taking my book to print for the second time. During this process, Celia Rocks and Dottie DeHart have provided publicity services that helped it become a bestseller on several business book lists, including the *Wall Street Journal*'s. Needless to say, I am thrilled with them. I urge any aspiring author to read—and heed—their advice.

> - Charles Garcia
>   Author of the *Wall Street Journal* bestseller,
>   *A Message from Garcia: Yes, You Can Succeed*,
>   published in English and Spanish

Writing a book? Then *101 Publishing Tips for Speakers & Consultants* should occupy a prominent spot on your desk. Packed with ignore-it-at-your-peril inside information, it will give you a whole new perspective on an industry that's unlike any other.

> - Alex Hiam
>   Author of *Marketing For Dummies*
>   and founder of www.insightsfortraining.com

I not only enjoyed reading the entire book (which is unusual for me), but I actually learned a lot, even after going through the publishing process three times. The book answers a lot of questions that cause authors (and would-be authors) needless confusion and anxiety. These days I meet regularly with successful people who want to write and publish books, and who don't have a clue, or who have the process totally mystified. This book is clearly their salvation.

- Morrie Shechtman
Author of *Working Without a Net: How to Survive and Thrive in Today's High Risk Business World, Fifth Wave Leadership: The Internal Frontier* and co-author of *Love in the Present Tense*

If you are a speaker or a consultant, having your own book is almost as critical as having your own business card. It will boost your credibility ten-fold—but only if it's well-written, well-designed and well-marketed. *101 Publishing Tips for Speakers & Consultants* will help you approach this daunting task with the confidence and the know-how that will ultimately take your business to the next level.

- Maribeth Kuzmeski
Author of *Red Zone Marketing: A Playbook for Winning All the Business You Want* and *85 Million-Dollar Tips for Financial Advisors*

You need this book. I guarantee that there is at least ONE tip in here that you don't yet know or don't yet understand—and that this one tip will either SAVE you from making a $10,000 blunder or enable you to EARN thousands of dollars more than you would have on your own.

> - Gregory J.P. Godek
> President of BestSeller Management and author of the bestseller *1001 Ways to Be Romantic*

Whether you're publishing your first book or your tenth, here's a wonderful resource that will help you get more mileage out of it than you ever thought possible. From settling on the right topic to hiring a good collaborative writer to understanding the sometimes-quirky publishing world, this book is jam-packed with sound advice for both the novice and the experienced writer. Celia Rocks and Dottie DeHart have covered an amazing amount of territory in this short, succinct, to-the-point offering. Kudos on a job well done!

> - Michele Borba, Ed.D.
> Author of *No More Misbehavin'* and *Don't Give Me That Attitude!*

Celia and Dottie have seen me through the publishing, marketing, and publicity of several books now. They have helped me achieve greater success than I ever dreamed possible, and along the way it was easy, fun, and enlightening. I wholeheartedly and without reservation endorse this book. Lots of practical wisdom lies within!

- Elaine Biech
  Author of *The Business of Consulting, The Consultant's Legal Guide, The Consultant's Quick Start Guide, Marketing Your Consulting Services* and *Training for Dummies*

If knowledge is power, *101 Publishing Tips for Speakers & Consultants* might as well come with a crown and a scepter. Not only do Rocks and DeHart teach you how to write a publishable book, they also teach you how to sell it once you've got it in hand. Now that's information you can really use.

- Mark Samuel
  Author of *The Accountability Revolution: Achieve Breakthrough Results in Half the Time*

Writing a book can accelerate your career. Selling your book, however, is far more complicated than selling a speech or a consulting project. Before you write another word, take the time to read *101 Publishing Tips for Speakers & Consultants*. Celia Rocks and Dottie DeHart guide you through the publishing maze. You'll avoid time-wasting mistakes and vastly improve your odds of writing a successful book.

- Chris Lytle
  Professional Speaker and
  Author of *The Accidental Salesperson*

Celia and Dottie have been distributing this wisdom to their clients for more than a decade. These two know what TO do and as importantly what NOT to do to get your book in your audience's hands.

- Kim DeMotte, Dr. NO
  Author of *The Positive Power of NO: How that little word you love to hate can make or break your business*

With *101 Publishing Tips for Speakers & Consultants*
Celia and Dottie have truly got their fingers on the pulse of
the industry—but more importantly to me, they also have
their hearts and souls there as well. This book is like getting
a Ph.D. in how-to!

> - Susie Galvez
>   Author of *InSPArations, Hello Beautiful:
>   365 Ways to Be Even More Beautiful, Weight
>   Loss Wisdom* and the *Ooh la la!* book series,
>   which includes *Perfect Face, Perfect Hair,
>   Perfect Makeup* and *Perfect Body*

Every business consultant wants to publish a book . . .
Having a book with your name on it opens new doors and
opportunities. However, the publishing field is very rough
on inexperienced authors. *101 Publishing Tips for Speakers &
Consultants* is the crash course you need to effectively break
into the publishing game. Don't call me unless you've read
it!

> - Mark Sankey, President
>   BRB Publications, Inc.
>   Facts on Demand Press

Foreword

I've always admired people who can put a lot of information into a small package. For any of you who have read my *1001 Ways to Market Your Books*, you know that I have trouble doing that. I always want to expand things, sometimes make them more complicated than they need to be. But Celia Rocks and Dottie DeHart avoided these errors in this new book.

Their 101 tips cover all the essential caveats, pointers and creative ideas that every speaker needs to know to write and publish a meaningful book—one that will further their careers rather than hinder them.

In my experience, the major error that new book authors make is that they stop too soon in promoting their books. Other things begin to pull for their attention, and soon, their book promotion efforts fall by the wayside.

I'm going to give you a basic rule—a rule that forbids excuses, a rule that will keep your book from falling by the wayside. I call it the *rule of five*.

All it takes is five promotions a day. Really, that's all it takes. Mail a letter. Send out a news release. Phone someone. Take an editor to lunch. Contact the media. It doesn't require much time—15 to 20 minutes is enough—but it can make a world of difference in how well your book sells.

There are five essential points for pursuing media exposure:

1. 85 to 90 percent of all news is planted. That means that most of the news you read in newspapers and magazines has come out of news releases sent to the media by businesses, associations, government offices and other organizations or individuals with something interesting (or not so interesting) to say.

2. If you can provide real news for the media, they will be glad to feature your book. That's why you should keep refining your news hooks until you find one that really meets a need. Don't send out a press release announcing any book until you can show that the book provides at least one benefit for potential readers—whether that benefit be entertainment, information, instruction, or enlightenment.

3. Follow up. Never assume that just because you sent someone a sample copy, they got it. There are three known Bermuda Triangles in New York City alone. There was a big semi sitting in the wilds of New Jersey with first class mail for more than two years (a real case!). There was a postman in Chicago who buried all his third class mail along with some first class mail (another real case!). If you learn only one rule of marketing, it is this: follow up, follow up, follow up.

4. Publicity begets more publicity. Once you get the ball rolling, it often will go on by itself. Local news features are often picked up by the wire services and spread across the country. Local radio and TV shows can lead to bookings on network shows. One or two features in the major review media, and soon every newspaper in the country is calling to ask for a review copy (or simply reprinting the review from one of the major sources).

5. If at first you don't succeed, try, try again. Persistence, above all, is the key to success in generating favorable publicity for your book. Believe in your book, keep on plugging away, and the reviews, interviews and articles will come.

No more excuses! If your book doesn't sell, there is only one reason (provided the book has any merit at all). And that reason is this: You're just plain lazy. If you spend just ten minutes a day, every day, on every book you publish, you will generate an incredible momentum for your book.

There are no reasons why any book should die after six weeks in the marketplace. Books, like diamonds, are forever—provided you are willing to put a little elbow grease behind their promotion and you use those ten minutes a day wisely.

Now get off your rear end and start doing your ten minutes a day right now. Don't wait. I mean it. Don't wait.

— John Kremer, author,
1001 Ways to Market Your Books

Introduction

"If only I had known."

Sometimes I wish I had a quarter for every time I've heard an author/client say those words! Writing a book is hard work, but that's not the real problem. It's the fact that all too often people gladly <u>do</u> the hard work—but then they mess up one obscure little detail that renders the hours of blood, sweat and tears virtually pointless.

Maybe they fail to hire a good proofreader before they go to press. Or they select a cover design that doesn't "pop." Or they choose a vanity publisher that's shunned by bookstores. Or they bungle a TV appearance because they didn't know to seek media training beforehand. The truth is, there's *a lot* to know about writing, publishing and marketing a book—and much of it falls under the category of "inside information."

During the many years we've been in business, Celia and I have heard many clients bemoan mistakes they've made with their books—mistakes that we could have prevented with a simple word of advice. And that's why we wanted to write this book: to help authors of future books make the choices that will increase their likelihood of success.

We've met a lot of wonderful, warm, talented people over the years, and this book is our way of saying "thank you" to them. I hope you will keep this copy on your desk and read it before you begin your next adventure in publishing—and that you'll never again have to say those five dreaded words: "*if only I had known.*"

Dottie DeHart

I. Concept

1. Not every idea is a book. Some are just magazine articles—or maybe booklets.

It is critical to know the difference. If you attempt to puff up your text to "make it into a book," the result will be what editors call "thin." Translate that as "weak," "strained," "forced," or even "hyped." Reviewers will quickly pick up on this over-reaching on your part, and either decline to review the book at all or weigh in with a negative review. On the other hand, a good, strong magazine article has tremendous value. Reprints of an article from a recognized national magazine can be sent to many individuals and companies who are current or prospective clients, with results that may be almost as powerful as what you might achieve with a whole book.

Then, too, what may work well is something bigger than a magazine article but smaller than a book—in short, a booklet. This may turn out as a saddle-stitched (stapled) publication in a book format with book-design features. For instance, it may have a cover just like a paperback book. It may not be salable in trade bookstores, but a booklet can be given away as a promotional piece, sold as part of a speaking engagement or workshop, or even sold via direct mail or via the web. Either a magazine article or a booklet also can serve as a foundation for building a full-scale book as you amass more facts and insights on your subject.

2. For a how-to book or a book that passes along your knowledge or experience, go with your BRILLIANCE.

There are many true experts out there on any number of subjects, so why risk going head to head with them unless you have genuine professional expertise? Write out of the solid core of your experience, out of the heart of what you do best. It will resonate on the pages of a book and win you the following you deserve. Anything less will ring hollow. (For more on this subject, see *Brilliance Marketing Management*, by Celia Rocks, Facts on Demand Press, Tempe, Arizona, 2003, or visit www.brilliancemarketing.com.)

3. Timing is everything.

What may make a best-selling book next year could well have been a flop last year. Catching the crest of the wave makes a material difference in book sales. If you can learn how to think 18 months ahead (two years ahead is even better), you can be golden.

Needless to say, this is extremely tricky business. The best editors in a category (whether in "business books" or "self-help" or whatever) frequently earn their reputations from how well attuned they are to trends that affect the book-buying public. What resources do you have that give you trend-setting insight in your field? Sometimes it's simply clear in your day-to-day work, but you have to be looking for the obvious.

Know Barnes & Noble's two burning questions.

The questions are really simple—but knowing the answers will be key to your success. Here are the questions:

1) Who is the reader for this book?
2) How will the reader know about this book?

He who tries to write for everybody may end up writing for nobody. Books have defined "publics." Know your prospective readers; be able to spell out their demographics and business or personal profiles as clearly as you can. Are you writing for baby boomers entering or nearing retirement? For political junkies who keep up with every new ripple in tax or environmental policy? For overweight females or underappreciated divorced males? Once you know who your readers are, determine how you can best—

and most economically—reach them. Will talk radio be your faithful ally? Or workshops in a rented Holiday Inn conference room? Or excerpts in the right in-crowd newsletters or magazines? When we were first starting out in the business, one of our clients had a book, *How to Find Anyone Who Was Ever in the Military*. It did well year after year because it understood its niche market and didn't try to do more than the title suggests.

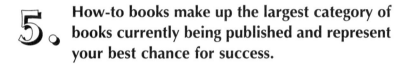

5. How-to books make up the largest category of books currently being published and represent your best chance for success.

If you can teach someone how to set up and run a home office, how to navigate the shoals of the in-between-marriages dating scene, or how to organize a local political campaign, there are people out there who will want your book.

It's easy to see why how-to books are so dominant in the marketplace. First of all, they belong to the nonfiction category, and nonfiction books sell more than fiction as a general rule. (There were only 3,500 or so novels published in 2002 out of some 130,000 books published overall.) Secondly, how-to ranges from cooking to crafts to home and garden titles to a broad range of business, self-help and alternative healthcare titles. Many, *many* books can legitimately be labeled "how-to."

Too many competing titles can choke a whole category.

Do your research in a large chain or independent bookstore to see what's been published in your niche over the last five or six years. Also scroll Amazon.com, books in print (those out and available to other readers), etc. Reference librarians can be remarkably helpful as you scan the competition. This sort of research is absolutely <u>essential</u> before you spend precious hours—by the score—in drafting your book, or thousands of dollars on a collaborating writer. You never know: someone already may have written just the book you have in mind. Or there may be too many books that are too close to what you want to do. In any event, a competitive analysis of titles in your niche is a key part of any viable book proposal. And if the market is crowded, your next question will be, how can I be different and stand out?

Study the bestsellers in your niche.

Make a list of their virtues. How are they organized? What cover and interior design features do you especially like? Who are their endorsers—and what kind of language is used in the endorsements?

Stylistically, how do they read? Is the language punchy? Colorful? Richly informative? Full of humor? Stories?

Notice how they use checklists, quizzes, floating quotes and other devices that complement the main text.

Do they have appendices with resource materials, such as lists of helpful suggested readings, audio and video tapes, websites? Do they employ an index? Do you want to emulate them or "knock their socks off" with something completely different?

8. A good how-to book should have "something old and something new."

In short, you need to summarize the best of what's already been written, then put forth enough original material to make your book striking. What you want is to build on the already existing wisdom about your subject, include it, but go beyond. Of course, it should all be woven together seamlessly and in a way that creates an impression of freshness, or new discovery.

9. Literary agents need books that sell big or authors who give evidence that they can write a multitude of books.

In other words, if you're an expert on a subject and have just one good book in you, and that book is likely to sell only 3,000-4,000 copies, you may have great trouble getting an agent. It will be easier for you to find a publisher on your own—or self publish.

10. Just because you get an agent does not mean you will get a publishing contract.

A good batting average for an agent is placing 70 percent of book projects accepted for representation. Many agents place only 60 percent or fewer of the manuscripts they take on. While your book is with an agent, it is "locked up." You will not be free to sell it on your own or to do anything else with it unless your agent gives you leave. Of course, you can always help your agent close a sale by proving to be an informed, high-energy author who understands long-term marketing.

11. The advance may be all the money you ever receive.

Roughly speaking, 75 percent of all books published are said to not "earn out" their advances. This means that if a publisher provides you, the author, with an advance of $9,000, unless you are in the fortunate 25 percent, that's the last nickel you'll ever get for your book. Your promised royalties will not materialize because sales of your book will not justify the house paying you any more than they've already shelled out. For this reason literary agents typically push for the largest advance possible, especially considering that the only money they make will be a 15 percent share of what comes to the author.

12. Traditional publishers may expect you to buy substantial quantities of your books.

Here you are, waiting for *them* to offer you a big advance, and there they are, waiting for *you* to agree to purchase 1,000 copies of your own books, at a 40 percent discount, to sell "in the back of the room." This expectation is becoming more and more common as publishers tighten down on the bottom line and seek to "guarantee" a book's breaking even well before the presses ever roll. Some publishers also may offer to provide your advance in books instead of cash. In point of fact, this actually can work out well for both sides. The publisher may give you a quantity of books that can translate into more money, once you sell them at full retail list price, than they would offer you in cash. And the books tendered to you this way also cost the publisher *less* than would doling out the hard cash. Take heart: Being offered the challenge of having to sell 1,000 copies of your own book can be a real positive. It will give you the chance to grow not only as an author but also as a promoter.

13. ISBN numbers belong to publishers and are purchased in groups of ten or more.

These numbers are secured from R.R. Bowker—P.O. Box 31, New Providence, New Jersey, 07974-9903, phone 888-269-5372—which publishes important databases and other essential statistics on virtually everybody who's anybody in the publishing industry. You can find them on the web at www.Bowker.com. Once you have ISBN numbers from Bowker, you are a book publisher, at least in name. With the acquisition of these numbers, however, comes a heavy responsibility to learn the ethics and protocol of publishing and to meet the expectations of both wholesale and retail buyers in the trade, and of course, the book-buying public. Becoming a publisher should not be done casually.

14. The book trade is set up to resist the "one-book publisher."

Self publishing seems to become more respectable after your third or fourth book. New self publishers often encounter the disdain of the big wholesale houses and bookstore chains, who lament the explosion of "one-book publishers" in the industry. Ingram now rejects publishers who have fewer than ten titles. Distributors, too, routinely refuse to take on a publisher who has not demonstrated a commitment to an ongoing program of issuing at least two or three books a year. If, however, you make your initial book an outright winner in content, cover design, title and endorsements, you will have done what you could to combat the stigma—and win over buyers in the trade. This is where your niche subject helps along with your ability to sell books via speaking engagements and consulting work such as workshops and seminars.

15. Most how-to books are best seen as high-class business cards.

While sales of your book may not make back your costs (as author or even as self publisher), do not give in to the temptation to consider it all a waste of money. We have found it to be quite the opposite for the majority of our clients. If you are good at what you do, a solidly-written and attractively-packaged book will open doors for consulting, workshops and speaking, and ultimately help build your business and your income. Highly successful consultants and other professionals understand this, and use their book as elegant business cards to grow their ventures. Consult your CPA on this, but normally all the money you invest in a book on your professional expertise (not, perhaps, on a hobby) should be a 100 percent tax-deductible business expense.

16. Publishing makes its money from a few books at the top of each season's list.

A mid-sized publisher doing, say, 40 books a year—15 "Springs" and 25 "Falls"—may have its sales breakdown as follows: perhaps two Spring and three Fall books will sell over 10,000 copies. One book, out of the whole year, may sell 50,000 or more. Money generated from these titles will keep the entire publishing program afloat. What the publisher hopes is that the majority of the other books will generate a modest profit for the house, or at least break even, and the books that actually lose money will be limited to a handful (five or six). For authors, however, the outlook is not so cheery. The sales picture described above means that out of the 40 books the house puts out that year, authors of just five books will do relatively well. The other thirty-five authors will have to make do with payments ranging downward from $1,500 or so twice a year to a few hundred dollars. And some will receive no royalty checks at all. Again, as a speaker or consultant, you do not have to "obsess" on this reality. Think of the book as a merchandisable tool to grow your income source, which is your speaking rate or consulting fee.

17. **Publishing demands patience.**

Authors sometimes carp about the time it takes publishers to decide to issue a contract for a book in which they are interested. This may be anywhere from six weeks to six months *after they have expressed an interest.* Then the wheels of book production and marketing seem to grind ever so slowly. This is because everything is scheduled to dovetail with editors' and graphic artists' availability, the most economical time to go to press (when a book can be "ganged" with other books of the same trim size for a lowest-dollar buy of paper), and the rigors of prepublication marketing. Normally speaking, a large or even mid-size publisher may take a year to get a book into the stores from the time the contract is signed. Some publishers block out an even longer "lead time"—fifteen or eighteen months or even a full two years. Small publishers can do it faster but they often sacrifice some benchmarks on the prepub marketing calendar, which then ends up costing them sales. If you decide to self publish, you will soon see how a process you thought would take you two weeks will instead take you two months. And so forth.

18. Only one book in ten from major publishers sells 10,000 copies or more. An average book issued by major publishers sells around 3,500 copies.

If the book is priced at $20 and an author has a contract to receive royalties of 10 percent on net sales (call this merely half the cover price, or $10), total author earnings would come to $3,500. That probably will not even cover the time you spent writing the book. If the book was self-published, and achieved the same quantity of sales in "the trade," it's likely that the author-publisher could reap two or three times that figure (after production costs were paid). If the author sold that quantity of books direct to consumers at full retail, the take would be $70,000, less production and marketing expenses. If you are a consultant and your day rate with a client is $3,500, or your workshop and keynote speaking rate is $7,500, you don't have to worry about how much you make from book sales. You should be more concerned that the right clients know about your book (which reflects your work) and are interested enough to consider hiring you.

19.

The impact of a speaker, trainer or workshop leader who has a book is considerably higher than that of a peer who does not have a book.

Consequently, your primary means of earning a living can be greatly enhanced simply because you have a book on the market—and available to sign and sell at full price after each talk or workshop. In a nutshell, your speaker's presentation should include important pieces from your book. Buying the book after your talk is how the audience "takes you home with them."

20.

Print on demand has had revolutionary implications for book publishers.

The quality of this digital process now approximates the look of pages printed on a traditional web press. Print on Demand (P.O.D.) can be a good way to run a test in a limited market (200-300 copies). It is also a way to keep books in print when it is no longer economical to warehouse 1,000 or more copies. However, neither reviewers nor bookstores are yet totally accepting of P.O.D. If a reviewer perceives that you have printed only 200 or so copies of a book, that reviewer is likely to pass on it. For them, you have not yet made a "serious" investment in publishing. If you don't believe in the book enough to print 2,000 copies, why, they ask themselves, should they believe in it enough to review it? Although we've become much more accepting of P.O.D. lately—it can be much more expensive per book (because you are printing a smaller quantity)—as one web press executive asked us, do you <u>really</u> need your book printed in two days? Proper planning will save you money.

II. Drafting

21. If you have a great idea for a nonfiction book, but feel you don't write well enough to be published, take heart! Collaborative writers and editors are available to help.

They can do wonders with your prose or with transcripts from tape-recorded sessions. Much that you already have on hand, in fact, can be grist for the mill: previously published articles, outlines and notes for workshops or speeches, memos (non-confidential) to clients or staff and so forth.

Insist on a collaborator who will work <u>hard</u> to capture your specific "voice." It's important that the book truly sounds like you. This will especially be true when you step up to the podium to deliver a talk to people who have already perused your book!

The collaborating writer/editor's personality also must be substantially in accord with yours if you are to work together productively. No, you do not need to be soul brothers or sisters, or "two peas in a pod," but there should be nothing about the writer that will irritate or jar you. Collaborating on a book is an intimate process and requires high trust and goodwill. In many instances of collaboration, lifelong friendships result.

Be sure that you discuss and agree upon whether the writer will be credited or not—and if so, in what way. Pure ghost writing (wherein the collaborating writer receives absolutely no credit) gives the illusion that an author wrote a book on his own when in fact someone else wrote it for him. Some collaborating writers may be content to have the author thank them in the Acknowledgments; some may want a line as editor on the copyright page; and still others may want to be listed on the front cover and title page as "with (name of collaborator)," or even share a byline, as: "Susie Brilliance (Main Author) and Linda Helper (Collaborating Writer)." It is especially appropriate to give the collaborating writer an "and" byline when she has in fact contributed substantial subject matter (facts, ideas, insights) to the book.

22. For nonfiction books, drafting the whole book before seeking a publisher can be counterproductive.

As a rule, what agents and editors want to see is a good book proposal. Sending in a 200-page finished manuscript for a nonfiction book marks you as a rank amateur. Proposals come in many forms; however, certain elements are virtually always a necessity. These are:

1. An overview or rationale which should answer the question: Why this book? And who are the readers?

2. A detailed chapter outline. One good format is a short, descriptive paragraph giving the essence of the chapter, followed by a series of bullet points of key pieces of the chapter.

3. A competitive analysis. This should provide a capsule summary of recent books similar to yours. In each case you should compare your book project to what's already been done, and show how your book goes considerably further or brings in original ideas or research beyond what's on the market so far.

4. One or two sample chapters. Often, editors like to see the first chapter plus an "interior" chapter (Chapter Five or Seven, for instance).

5. A biographical sketch on you as the author. Highlight previous books, published articles, workshop and/or speech-circuit experience, professional work background and degrees.

6. A marketing plan. What are you prepared to do to get out and make your book sell? This is where you can talk about previous appearances on TV and radio, interviews with you published in newspapers and magazines and other examples of marketing your material to the public. We have found that if you are a speaker and can "guarantee" that you will be speaking three to four times a month on the book's subject, that information will certainly interest a publisher.

One good tip for book proposals is "lead with your strongest element." If, for example, your competitive analysis reveals that there is a major gap in the research or elucidation of a subject, and your book will fill it, you may want to start the proposal right there. If you have already been on national TV—and have an entrée to get back on—that is a very strong starting point.

On the matter of return postage, a good idea is to enclose a simple self-addressed and stamped number 10 envelope for the agent's or publisher's reply. On the proposal itself, you can put this note: *Rather than return, please put into recycling.* It'll cost you less to print out another pro-posal for your next submission than pay return postage. And that way each proposal you send is crisp and clean.

23. Are you enamored of the idea of "being an author?" Or are you ready to put in the sweat equity of writing the book?

Even working with a collaborating writer will require a considerable expenditure of time, energy—and money. It doesn't cost much to throw a raw (weakly-written or poorly-edited) copy into typesetting and turn out 200 copies of a book with print on demand. But this is what is termed "vanity publishing," and it's what has caused major players in the book trade to shy away from subsidized and self-published books. To arrive at a finished book that matches up to the best of what the New York publishers put out . . . now THAT'S another matter.

Good collaborating writers and editors will charge any-where from $75 to $100 an hour (some well-known writers may charge even more). Freelance line and copy editors may range from $50, and proofreaders may be a bit less, from $25 an hour. In some instances, editors may charge by the page, with higher rates to edit technical rather than general writing.

Furthermore, a few editors prefer to give clients a ball-park project figure. This has its perils, as perhaps the time and effort required to make something into a publishable manuscript might go beyond the $3,000, $7,500, or $12,000 figure originally agreed upon. Then a writer may end up either shortchanging himself—or shortchanging the project. It is <u>not</u> necessarily cheaper to have a writer work with you to redraft a book that you have written weakly than to have the writer collaborate with you right from the start.

24. Learning to write professionally requires discipline, coaching and lots of practice.

Colleges, community colleges and some ad-hoc writing schools offer courses in various levels of nonfiction writing. Get the best references you can before signing up for a class (and an excellent reference is book or magazine publication by former students). Online one-on-one tutorials also abound these days. There are plenty of resources available to sharpen your writing skills. To learn how to write, there's nothing like writing—every day, if you can block out the time—and then having a qualified writing coach give you feedback and tips for improving. Good writing takes time, and for many speakers and consultants, verbalizing your book into a tape recorder and having it transcribed for use by a ghostwriter makes much more sense.

25. Know who your readers are—and write directly to them.

Trying to talk to the whole world is difficult. You'll find it much easier to write if you can envision your readership—entrepreneurs, salespeople, retirees, whomever it might be. And write as if you were standing in front of a group of them and sharing your ideas or describing a process that could benefit them. Imagine their questions—and respond to them! If you can round up some members of your target niche, by all means try to get them to read a chapter draft or two. This kind of feedback will prove invaluable.

26. If you want to be a writer, be a reader.

From time immemorial, teachers of writing have laid down this maxim. Authors who write books or essays on their artistic life inevitably reinforce this piece of advice. You will dodge it at your own peril. What, then, should you read? You can never go wrong with the classics, from Shakespeare to Emerson to Hemingway to National Book Award winners such as Saul Bellow and Toni Morrison. Anthologies of great American poetry, essays and short stories also can be wonderful models for adroit crafting of language. Then, of course, read your competition—authors who have successfully published in your niche. You're not there to "steal" from them, but you will need to take their ideas into account, and go beyond what they encompass, offering a new twist on an old model or proposing an entirely original approach.

27. For how-to books, be appropriately prescriptive, not namby-pamby.

Experts should write with authority. Gently but firmly tell the reader what to do in order to achieve this or that result. As in, "If you want to be a writer, be a reader" and "Sales comes easier to those who rise early and get out there. So don't lie in bed past 6 a.m. Be 'up and at 'em.'" Avoid such beating-around-the-bush phrasing as, "In the normal course of things, it's a good idea to . . . " and, "Whenever possible, try your best to . . . " You get the idea.

28. Write for women. If you do that well, men will be happy to read you too.

This is an old adage of newspaper feature writing. The idea here is that women are more "relational" than men, and often more taken with colorful details and narrative flow. Writing that appeals to readers' interest in the way characters interact, as well as writing that delves into the concrete specifics of a scene or a situation will simply be more alive, more interesting than a dull recitation of facts.

Men, too, like this kind of writing—so you certainly won't *lose* any readers if you keep your female readership in mind as you draft your book.

29. Do not fill up your book quoting other people's books and essays. You yourself must "be the expert."

Yes, it's okay to mention Tom Peters or Harvey Mackay or whichever other stars you like in a field such as marketing, and even quote them—a *little*. Do not, however, make your book simply a pastiche of excerpts from other people's books or ideas. YOU must be the authority—and the star— in your own how-to book. If you need to summarize ideas in the field, then summarize, but without sprinkling your text with one name after another of other authors and their ideas. When writers quote a competitor rather than developing their own "brilliant ideas," they miss the opportunity to be "quotable."

30. When giving cases, use some dialogue. Bring your cast of characters alive.

Readers of how-to books understand that when you use quotes, you are approximating what might actually have been said. No one expects court-transcription accuracy—just get the sense of the conversation right. If you are using actual true cases, as opposed to cases you invented as examples, you should of course run the final draft by the subjects you are quoting and get them to approve of the cases, quotes and all. If they suggest changes, make them, or at least dialog with the subject until you come to agreement. Using quotes is good "show, not tell" composition. Often, indirect quotes can be converted to direct quotes to liven up a passage. You may have written:

Jake told his son Jeff that building a tree house together was a great bonding exercise and that more Dads and their kids ought to try it.

This can become:

"Jeff, do y'know what? Building this tree house together, you and me, has been great. I think it's brought us closer, don't you? More Dads and their kids ought to try it!"

31. Own a copy of Strunk. Read it. Re-read it. Wear it out reading it.

If you got through school without being introduced to *The Elements of Style,* by William Strunk Jr. and E.B. White, rush out today and get yourself a copy. If you are already savvy to "Strunk," be sure to page through this little book periodically and refresh your memory. Every word in Strunk's book counts, whether in the section on "elementary rules of usage," or that on "principles of composition," or the one on "misused words and expressions." Absorbing and applying Strunk's guidelines is guaranteed to make you a better writer—or editor. A few samples of Strunk:

Make the paragraph the unit of composition.
Put statements in positive form.

Example:
Weak: *He was not very often on time.*
Strong: *He usually came late.*

Use definite, specific, concrete language.
Weak: *A period of unfavorable weather set in.*
Strong: *It rained every day for a week.*

Strunk was E.B. White's writing teacher at Cornell. White must have learned something useful about language, for he went on to become one of America's great twentieth-century essayists. White closes the book with his own essay on style. In that piece he has some trenchant advice on topics such as overblown, pompous writing, ways to achieve clarity, how to cut out weak qualifiers (such as *rather, very, little, pretty*), and the art of revision.

32. First lines and first paragraphs count big. Hook 'em or lose 'em.

Going back to the Ancients of Greece and Rome, rhetoric has always held that the first words of any piece of writing were points of great emphasis. How you open your Introduction and the first chapter of your book may make the difference between acceptance or rejection by a publisher—or by a browser in the bookstore. Acquisition editors who pore over proposals and manuscripts looking for a gem often confine their initial search to the first page or three of a submission. If those forty or fifty lines of prose hold their interest, they will read further. If not, they reject the entire project and move on. Consumers in your local bookstore often behave in exactly the same way.

Here is the opening paragraph of *Writing Down the Bones: Freeing the Writer Within* by Natalie Goldberg:

I was a goody-two-shoes all through school. I wanted my teachers to like me. I learned commas, colons, semicolons. I wrote compositions

*with clear sentences that were dull and boring.
Nowhere was an original thought or genuine
feeling. I was eager to give the teachers what I
thought they wanted.*

Can't you just see little Natalie, dress perfectly pressed, hair combed and black patent leather shoes neatly crossed as she laboriously adheres to the rules of grammar? You can relate to her image of the eager-to-please "teacher's pet," either because you were one or you knew one. You instantly realize that the advice in the book is going to be the antithesis of the dull and boring lessons from fifth-grade English class—and you're compelled to read on.

33. In describing a process or building an argument, don't skip a step.

Coherence is another critical element in composition. Readers expect you to take them by the hand and lead them through an explanation of a process, or a line of reasoning, step by step. We all have a certain built-in logic, and it is to this innate sense of order that writers must appeal. Technical writers become masterful at coherence because they are forever describing a process of assembly or repair or retooling, and the success of those working concretely with machine parts depends upon how clear the writers have been in giving them the step by step. Nonetheless, coherence is important for less technical processes too. Psychologists working with a couple in marriage counseling, for instance, must take great pains to help each party see his or her role in the unraveling of a relationship, and what amends and adjustments must be made to put things back together. And if you miss a step . . . the whole process of healing can be compromised or aborted.

A good test of coherence is reading a passage out loud to people who are part of your target readership. Ask them to listen, follow and tell you if they "get" the process. If having heard your reading, they can give the process back to you in their own words, you're home free. As a consultant or speaker, you know how important it is to take a "step back" before you get to the "ah ha" moment.

34. Lists with bullet points are welcome—no, virtually essential—in the how-to book.

Bullet points excel in helping readers comprehend a list of goals, a list of options, or even a list of steps in a how-to process. Numbers do this as well, and depending on the situation, numbers may even be preferable to bullet points (as was the case with our listing of elements in the book proposal, p.19). Like constructs, diagrams, charts and the like, bullet points also prove striking and reassuring to browsers. They may be one of the points of attraction in a text for your prospective book buyer as she leans against a wall at Borders to page through your work.

Here, used with permission, is an excellent example of bullet pointing from Tom Woll's book *Publishing for Profit* (Chicago: Chicago Review Press, 1998):

What Do You Want to Be?

The first key to establishing and running a successful publishing company is to define your editorial niche. Ask yourself the following questions—and be sure to answer them truthfully:

- *In what subjects will your company specialize?*
- *Why?*
- *What makes your books unique within the market?*
- *Do you have particular expertise within this market?*
- *Do you know who the expert authors are? Can you reach them?*
- *Who are your competitors within this subject category?*
- *What stores carry the kind(s) of books you'll publish?*
- *Where in the store is the category placed?*
- *What are the attributes of competitive books?*

> *Size*
> *Price points*
> *Hardcover or paperback*
> *Number of pages*
> *Use of color*

- *What is the average number of copies sold within this category?*
- *If you sell this many, will your profitability goals be met?*
- *If not, how many new books will you have to sell to be profitable?*
- *How many new titles within the category are published seasonally?*
- *Are sales in the category expanding or are they contracting?*
- *How will you distinguish those titles you plan to publish?*
  > *Editorial content*
  > *Size or format*
  > *Price*
  > *Color*
  > *Author*

35. Have a rough page count in mind as you write.

Books have a range of ideal page lengths, depending on the niche. Simplicity books, as a rule, tend to be small (94-

160 pages). Leadership titles rarely run under 200 pages and often are closer to 300. Whatever your niche, pay attention to competing titles and be "in the ballpark" for things such as trim size, page count and price. Writing a book that is either much smaller or much bigger than most titles in your niche will decrease the likelihood of a successful sale. Drafting also may be helped by your having a trim size in mind, so you can envision how the words will lay out on a book page. Be aware, however, that traditional publishers will have the final say on trim size. If you are a self publisher, choose a size that is common to your market niche.

III. EDITING

36. Editing can be broken down into types— and each type is important.

All editing is not the same. *Acquisition editors* are literary scouts who cast their nets into their fields of specialization and "sign" authors to write books for the publishing house. These are the editors to whom you must appeal with your book proposal, sample chapters and marketing plan. Some acquisition editors also edit, when they can grab the time to do it, and some do not. *Developmental editors* are book architects. They can work with a specialist in a field to generate a classy, professional text, either right from the start of a project or else in reshaping an early draft. Such editors, typically, are good writers themselves and can coach writing, perform heavy editing, or rewrite sections or whole chapters. They are adept at spotting elements that are missing or out of place and seeing to it that these elements are either created or put in their proper slots. Many traditional publishers no longer work with authors on developmental editing; if a submission does not arrive at a publisher in good shape, it will simply be rejected. *Line editors* are careful readers and walking dictionaries (and sometimes encyclopedias) who have a nose for spotting errors, whether in grammar, tone or fact, and who are geniuses in word choice and readability. Normally speaking, the changes they recommend will be line by line. *Copy editors* are similar to line editors, except they will frequently not be as in-depth in their general knowledge and will focus more on grammar, punctuation and spelling. *Proofreaders* are a subset of copy editors—those who stand in the breach between page proofs and finished printed books. They often get the proofs close to the deadline for running 10,000 copies and must catch any and all remaining errors before glitches show up in bookstores coast to coast and embarrass both publisher and author.

37. How to guarantee your manuscript will land in the slush pile.

It is really quite simple to achieve this less-than-welcome destination for your book project. Just do your book entirely on your own, with no more feedback or editing than your spouse and your next-door neighbor might provide. Send in a finished manuscript cold to a number of publishers without looking at their catalogs or any of their previous books, and without seeking out and following their submission guidelines. To fortify their inclination to reject your book, phone editors at the publishing house and use up their valuable working time listening to you rave about how original and wonderful your manuscript is and demand that they give it their full attention.

38. Good books are the work of many hands.

The idea that authors singlehandedly create monumental works of nonfiction is a myth. Nine times out of ten, an author will have benefitted from the ideas and critiques of a half-dozen or more people, some of them professional writers or editors. Major suggestions typically come from peers in the field. This is all to the good. Books are better when a number of heads come together to rethink, reshape and polish a manuscript. We recommend that you spend $1,000 and send your "final" book to four associates in your field, paying them each $250 to read and comment on your work.

39. Some texts need to be "exploded from within."

Many times a book can be justifiably made larger by finding passages that simply summarize or offer a very general description of a process, then coaxing out the specifics and enlarging that section of the book. This is what Patrick Grace of Publisher's Place calls "exploding a text from within." Be careful: this is different from just puffing up a text with throwaway fluff. The specifics must be important and must make a real contribution to whatever passage you seek to "explode." This process falls within the domain of developmental editing. Most commonly, the editor will notice the need for more detail, then coach the author on writing the material. Or the editor may take raw information the author provides and work it into the text.

40. The key adjective is "publishable."

This is a true "shop-talk" term. People on the outside of the publishing industry rarely hear this term, much less use it. What's meant by "publishable" is that a manuscript has enough originality and usefulness to appeal to a segment of the book-buying public so that somewhere there exists a publisher who would likely issue a contract to buy it—if only that publisher can be identified by the author or an agent.

A "publishable" manuscript may nonetheless be rejected numerous times. Here are some of the reasons for rejection that have nothing to do with the quality of the book project:

- A suitable publisher has recently issued, or has under contract, a work that is too similar to the submitted manuscript.
- There has been a change of chief editors in a publishing house and the new chief editor has a slightly different taste in books than his predecessor—or simply wants to chart new territory.
- The house would like to buy the manuscript but is over budget already that year for acquisitions.
- A publisher may not believe that the author will be energetic or "high profile" enough in doing signings and media appearances and otherwise promoting the book.

41. Most acquisition editors barely have time to edit during their normal working hours.

Authors and would-be authors sometimes think that editors are hard to reach because they are so engrossed in their editing that they cannot look up and answer the phone. Actually, most editors cannot grab the phone because most of the day they are in sales, marketing or editorial meetings, or they are already on the phone with agents and the house's existing authors. A common complaint among editors is that they have to flee the premises in order to find the peace and quiet to edit—normally, this means working at home on, say, Wednesdays—with a standing order that they will take no phone calls.

42. As an unpublished author, you don't fit into an editor's workday.

If you've absorbed the spirit of the entry just above, you will see why you and your work are not part of an editor's daily program. Any number of publishers may declare that, "We welcome new authors." What that means is, "We're already working with sixty authors we like, and we may be open to adding five to ten new authors this year." So if your proposal fits neatly into the book category they are already looking for—and if the proposal shows promise of your being able to deliver an original, classy and salable book—they will get back to you. First, though, the editors at that house must batten down all the hatches relating to their current publishing projects. So it may take a while for any of them to read your proposal. Bear in mind, too, that your proposal is in competition with fifty others that have arrived the same month—and yours must be the best.

43. At major publishing houses, the editor whom you deal with to arrive at a contract may not be the editor who edits your book.

That is because many publishers these days do not have enough line editors or copy editors on staff to handle the manuscripts they put under contract. Thus, many manuscripts are shipped out to places such as Lawrence, Kansas, or Phoenix, Arizona, where editorial production companies or solo freelancers working from home perform the editing.

44. Good editing will assure that your best ideas are delivered in the most attractive wrapping.

There is no question about it: many books that garner wonderful reviews and end up selling big in their niches owe a debt to one or more editors. The difference between the manuscript the author turns in and the finished text of a published book can be much greater than is popularly imagined. Developmental editors worth their salt can do any, or all, of the following for a manuscript:

- ✓ Rearrange chapters to create a more enticing "flow"
- ✓ Collapse two or more chapters into one to avoid redundancy or cut marginal matter
- ✓ Conceive of entirely new chapters that the author (working with the editor) should create
- ✓ Reorganize the flow of paragraphs *within* a chapter
- ✓ Tighten the writing, dynamize the writing by suggesting stronger verbs and nouns and thinning out clutches of adjectives and adverbs, and introduce more dialog and other colorful touches to bring a book to life.

45. Good editing also will project your own "voice," though it may be a more cultivated voice, and your authority.

Beware of editors who want to "write their own stuff" into your book. This can be dangerous power tripping. You are the expert behind the content and your reputation will rise or fall according to the accuracy and insightfulness of the information you convey in your book. Editors are there to help you with questions of literary architecture, deft phrasing, smooth flow and so forth. If they have a suggestion for content, they should feel free to make it. But you must be the judge of whether an insight that comes from an editor belongs in your book or not.

46. Titles and subtitles are key to a book's success—and editors often have the final say.

A book title is no small item. The right title can make the difference between a book selling 3,000 copies—and 30,000 copies. Authors may not always have the best title on their manuscript for marketability's sake. That is why editors often have the task of either stamping their approval on the title proposed by the author, or negotiating with him or her to change it to something snappier or trendier.

As a rule, titles that promise benefits work well: *The 7 Habits of Highly Successful People, Swimming with the Sharks, Up the Organization, Organizing the Good Life*. Subtitles often can take over where the main title leaves off. A subtitle can be longer, and can spell out even more benefits, as Grace Associates did for Colonel Hal Shook's work, *Flying Spirit*, by making the subtitle read: *A Leader's Guide to Creating Great Organizations*.

The shorter the main title the better—in most cases, two or three words are ideal. Occasionally, though, a long title rings a bell with book buyers, as did *Everything You Always Wanted to Know About Sex—But Were Afraid to Ask*. Bookstore managers—if you can get their ear for a few seconds amid their typically whirlwind days—can be excellent for giving you feedback on prospective titles.

IV: DESIGN

47. For cover design, rely on graphic artists who specialize in book covers.

Whoever said, "You can't judge a book by its cover," has never attempted to sell a book to the category buyers at Borders or Barnes & Noble. Covers are HUGELY IMPORTANT for successful book sales. Experienced wholesale buyers have very clear taste parameters for what constitutes a good, or even an acceptable, cover. Graphic artists who are experienced in trade book cover design will be worth the money. The low end of book cover design? Around $1,000. The upper limits can reach $3,000.

48. Beware of authors, yourself or someone else, who think they can design a book cover just as well as they can write the book.

Most traditional publishers will not welcome your pressing hand-drawn designs upon them. And if you are a self publisher, you cannot spend money any better than enlisting a real pro to design your cover for you. He or she will start with your ideas but will use them as a takeoff point toward something that will meet the expectations of Barnes & Noble, Borders and other major booksellers.

On the other hand, an author needs to be happy with the cover, for he or she is going to be everywhere showcasing the book. Unhappy authors make bad salespeople.

49. Covers run in vogue.

Pay attention to what's in the stores. For awhile, a white background was considered the most chic choice for a cover. A number of New York publishers seem to have developed a prejudice against green as a dominant color for book covers. The reasons for this are mysterious, but be advised: Use green with caution and only for an effect you have determined you absolutely need to have.

50. Does your cover "pop" from across the room?

Place the prospective cover for your book on a wall at eye level and step back at least 12 feet. If title, author's name and the main images of the cover are striking at this distance, the cover can be said to "pop." Chances are you've got a powerful cover. If not, and you're a self-publisher, keep trying. (Or, if you have a traditional publisher and they've sent you a cover for review, push *them* to do better.)

There's also the one-inch test. Reduce your cover to one-inch tall and paste it into a magazine column with text top and bottom, as if it were part of a review. See how well your cover "pops" at that size. If it has punch at just one inch high, it'll have punch at full size.

Another trick is wrap your cover around a book the same size as yours and put it up, front cover out, on a shelf of books at home (or better yet, in a bookstore), and see how it does next to competing covers. If a store manager or assistant manager is handy, ask him or her for an opinion on how your cover looks on the shelf.

51. The purpose of the front cover is to get browsers to turn the book over and read the back cover.

Your front cover is everybody's first impression of your book.

For buyers at the chains, your cover has about five seconds to be a hit or a flop, for that's all they're likely to give it. The same may well be true of browsers in the bookstores.

If a browser likes a cover, there's a fair chance that he or she will flip the book over and look at the back cover.

52. The back cover counts big—as does the dust jacket copy.

The back cover is where people, generally speaking, will begin to read your book. They'll read the blurb, the endorsements and the author's bio, and look at the author's picture. The purpose of the back cover is to get browsers to open the book and begin to look inside. And what is the first thing they will see when they open the book? If there is a dust jacket, they'll look at the inside front cover copy . . . followed soon thereafter by the inside *back* cover copy!

Make sure these most important "selling areas" are well written. If you don't feel that the copy presented to you is fresh and compelling, ask your publisher (or whoever wrote it) to give it another shot. It might even be worth your while to hire a professional copywriter—someone who regularly "sells with words"—to do the job. You can find these intrepid souls working for advertising or public relations agencies, or often, working freelance for fairly reasonable rates.

53. Don't forget the "shelving category."

This usually goes at the top left or right hand side of the back cover, often underlined. Barnes & Noble has its own list of shelving categories and it's helpful to march along with that list. If a book spans two separate categories, you can usually include both, separated by a slash. Example:

Self-Help/Simplicity
Small Business/Marketing
Alternative Health/Weight Loss

54. The spine is a critical and sometimes slighted aspect of the design process.

Ninety-nine percent of the time, the way your book will be displayed in a bookstore is "spine out." All a browser will notice at first glance is that spine, with letters he has to crook his neck to read. Make sure the spine typeface is large enough, stands out clearly against the background and conveys the essentials: Title, key words from the subtitle (if possible), author's full name (if possible) and publisher's colophon. It's nice to get a four-color image on the spine if you can fit it in, letting some attractive detail "spill over" from the front cover.

55. Interior art—photos, line drawings, constructs—can have major impact.

If you page through how-to books at your local store, you probably will be struck by the number, and quality, of interior illustrations. Whether these images are charts, graphs, diagrams, constructs, line drawings or photos, they inevitably liven up a book. They need not be great in number. Often just five or six good images in a book will be enough. When browsers scan pages, they come upon these images, and, if the images are well executed, the browser almost certainly will treat the prospective purchase more seriously.

V. PRODUCTION

56. Don't move far from the predominant trim size and price points in your category.

Business books, for instance, are commonly 6 x 9 or 5.5 x 8.5. Hardcovers usually go for anywhere from $21.95 to $25.95, trade softcovers from $11.95 to $15.95. There may be exceptions, but be cautious. You always do best staying within the parameters already established in a given niche.

57. Print less your first run.

Unless you KNOW you can sell 3,000 or 5,000 copies, print fewer—say 2,000 or even 1,500. You can always go back to press for more. Spend the money you'll save on more promotion. People will think, *For only $1,200 more I can get another 1,000 copies*. But do you NEED that extra 1,000 copies now?

There are other good reasons to print fewer copies. There's always something to fix after a first run. Let's say you find a glaring error after a book comes back from the printer. Wouldn't you rather have that error in circulation on 1,500 copies instead of 3,000? Or maybe you've secured some late endorsements that are terrific, or a great review by a major reporter. Either would help your back cover. Now you can fix the glitch and slip in that glowing big-name endorsement or upbeat review. *Improve, improve, improve!*

58. People go ga-ga about "print overseas and save big bucks." Well, not quite.

Yes—if you have a book with 84 four-color plates, by all means shop around in Singapore, Hong Kong, or South Korea. Normally, however, you can do fine with black and white closer to home. Shipping costs will be much lower and so will turnaround time.

59. Print with book printers, not the printer down the street who "once in awhile" does a book.

Book printers are those who base at least half of their total business on printing books. Often they have been in operation for decades, turning out thousands of books for publishers of all sizes. They know what they are doing. They have learned how to achieve good professional book quality, keep costs down, give customers good "turnaround time" (four to five weeks), protect books in shipment and many other things. If something goes wrong with a printing job, they will redo it. They are your best bet for printing your book.

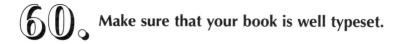 Make sure that your book is well typeset.

An important publishing decision is the choice of "body type" for a book, along with a compatible "chapter head" type, point size and "leading." If you are a self-publisher, this is your responsibility, though good book printers can be immensely helpful in advising you. A reasonable choice for most how-to books is a typeface in the Garamond family, 11 points high with a minimum of two points "leading" (white space between the lines), or what in the trade is referred to as "11 on 13." Even more generous leading is advisable, say 11 on 14 or even 11 on 15. Some typefaces "print big;" if you are working with such a face, ten-point type might be fine, leaded two or three points. If your trim size is slightly oversized, for instance 6 x

9, you may want to go with 12-point type—and generous leading.

Besides Garamond, other faces that have been used effectively in book printing include Bodoni, Bookman, Caledonia, Electra and Nebraska. (This book, for example, is printed in 12-point Goudy on 18-point leading.) Also on the subject of typesetting, take care that the margins on each page are generous enough to look professional and promote readability. Guard especially against inadequate margins in "the gutter" (the interior margins on each page); otherwise, you'll force readers to have to "read into the gutter" on left-facing pages.

61. Books are printed in signatures.

A signature is a group of pages, sixteen in all. Thus, the total number of pages in a given book will typically be a multiple of sixteen, as, for instance, 160, 176, 192, 208, 222, etc. This may not equate to the last page number in a book. "Front matter"—from title page through the last page of the introduction—is often numbered with Roman numerals (iii, iv, v, etc.) and not all pages have a page number. It is possible to use a half-signature (eight pages) as part of a book if a full signature is not needed at the end; there is usually, however, no savings in cost of paper, which is to say a printer will charge the same for a half-signature as for a full one. We recommend that authors use extra pages in the back of the book to sell their seminars, workshops, speaking and other products and services.

62. "Galleys" are still necessary, but perhaps in smaller quantities.

Except now they are simply page proofs, even though called "bound galleys." They should be stamped "Uncorrected Page Proofs." Another possible stamp is: "For Review." Don't put "Not for Sale" on the stamp, because it sounds adversarial.

What is the purpose of galleys? They are prepared for anyone who needs an early version of your book, say, long-lead magazines and trade publications such as *Library Journal* and *Publishers Weekly*.

VI. MARKETING

63. Many times, authors think that traditional publishers will "do it all for me."

Instead, there usually is a wave of publicity for the book that gets written before the book is published and whose release is timed to coincide with the book's arrival in stores. This wave, if you're lucky, may last six weeks. Then the book is on its own.

Unless you are one of the superstar "top-of-the-list" authors in a given publishing house, you will find that soon after your book hits the bookstores, 90 percent of the marketing will depend upon YOU! So have a good author's marketing plan in place, and be ready to roll. The PR *oomph!* that counts will likely depend more upon your efforts than on what the publisher may have done for you.

64. Finding a good publicist is an art in itself.

To increase publicity, some authors may choose to work with a publicist or a public relations firm, but finding a good one can be tricky. A compatible publicist will share the same realistic hope that you have and will be willing to work hard. If you find someone who is a hard worker, understands your ultimate goals for the book and has the experience and creativity to make something happen, you will have succeeded in your search. How do you know a publicist has what it takes to get you and your book into the limelight? By her track record.

Here are some questions you may ask of a publicist: *How many books have you worked on? How many have you handled in my niche?* (Different publicists specialize in different niches, just like editors and literary agents.) *What was right with the best book you ever worked on? What was wrong with the worst book you ever worked on?* Publicists, like everyone else, learn from their mistakes. So ask her: *What have you learned from yours?*

65. Even a great publicist cannot overcome a bad book—or a book that has lost its window of opportunity in the market.

If your book is nothing more than a rehash of what's already "out there"—*same old, same old,* in other words—a publicist is not going to be able to rescue you. Ditto if your book needs a close relationship to trends in the country or in the news, and the "moment" for your book has come and gone. Rocks-DeHart had a contract to publicize a Y2K book (remember that period—when we were expecting the whole world to come crashing to a halt?). The book, however, was late—published in December 1999. (This book should have been published by October.) By the time the book had settled onto bookstore shelves, there was no time for the media or the consumer to react to the book. Soon thereafter, the clock struck midnight, and it was clear that the much-feared Y2K crisis was not going to happen. Another "bad timing" example: There once was a book on how to stay happily married, written by a counselor, and as the book was coming onto the market our not-so-happily married counselor/author was getting a divorce. So much for that book's marketability, no matter how good the blurbs and press releases might have been!

66. You can expect a publicist to read a good portion of your book before you hire her.

Before the publicist has been hired, you can expect him or her to read one or two chapters of your book. If your prospective partner in promotion will not commit to doing that, there is a problem. After letting the publicist have a couple weeks with your book, here are some questions you can ask: *What did you learn from my book? What breakthrough information have you found in my book? What kind of readers do you think my book will appeal to? How do you propose to reach those readers? If you were to pitch my book to the media right now, what is the most interesting hook we have?*

If the publicist stumbles all over the answers to these questions, move on. You have not yet found the right person to pitch your book.

67. A good publicist will find the feature stories in your book.

A decent nonfiction book ought to contain at least one, if not two or three, feature stories per chapter. A savvy publicist has the eye to spot these stories immediately, just as a decorator knows where to put the coffee table. These are the stories a publicist needs to ferret out and sell to the media. The more legitimate stories the publicist can locate and serve up as articles, interviews, or at least good "sound bites," the better the run your book is likely to have. These stories, by the way, are the *real* news—not the fact that your book has come out. Nobody makes a to-do about a magazine coming out or a newspaper. A book (unless it's a book by a celebrity) is no different. What's news is the breakthrough information or insights *in* the book, not the appearance of the book itself.

68. The press release is your leading publicity instrument.

There is really far too much to say about press releases to do justice to the subject in a book like this one. However, you do need to understand that a good press release functions as a sort of "CliffsNotes™" for editors. It provides a greatly condensed overview of what your book is all about. And because very few editors have the time to read your book cover to cover, a concise, informative, well-written press release is critically important.

As was mentioned in the last tip, the fact that you have a new book out is not news. That's why your press release must center on the valuable information in your book—valuable information that makes a good story. Oh, by the way, if there are 20 great stories in your book, you may ultimately need 20 separate releases. One story at a time: that's the rule for press releases! Here's a sample press release:

WILEY
News

For Immediate Release

For a review copy of the book
or an interview with the author,
please contact Dottie DeHart,
Rocks-DeHart Public Relations,
at 828-459-9637 or DSDeHart@aol.com

Seize the Mentoring Moment!

No doubt about it, mentoring is in. According to entrepreneur and new Wall Street Journal
*best-selling author Charles Garcia, successful business people don't wait
for the company to provide a mentor—they find their own.*

New York, NY (December 2003)—Once upon a time, greed and ruthless ambition ruled

the Halls of Business. Maybe not *really*, maybe not in every case, but such was the common

perception. You made it to the top of the corporate ladder by climbing on the backs of others. If

someone seemed to be gaining on you, well, you crushed their fingers under your $300 shoes.

After all, it was a dog-eat-dog, every-man-for-himself world. Fortunately, says Charles

Garcia—owner of Sterling Financial Group, one of the fastest-growing, most successful

companies in America—that attitude has changed. Instead of stepping on a colleague's

outstretched fingers, successful business people are more likely to extend a helping hand.

Mentoring. According to Garcia, author of the new *Wall Street Journal* Business

Bestseller *A Message from Garcia: Yes, You Can Succeed* (2003, John Wiley & Sons, ISBN:

0-471-44893-1, $24.95), it's the hallmark of a kinder, gentler business world and a boon for any

"newbie" long on drive and determination but short on experience. There's only one caveat: with

budgets stretched to the limit and many companies wondering how to even make payroll, formal

mentoring programs are the exception, not the rule. But if you're an aspiring mentee, don't let

that stop you.

111 River Street • Hoboken, NJ 07030

"Too many people think of mentoring as a structured, 'official' arrangement," explains Garcia. "That's a misconception. If you want to benefit from a mentor, you must take the initiative to seek the advice and wisdom of people you admire. Volunteer for projects that allow you to collaborate with them. Take them to lunch and ask them questions. Ask if you can 'shadow' them at work and see what they do. Just pay close attention when you're around them. Today's mentee is not a passive recipient of knowledge; he or she is an active participant in the mentoring process."

Garcia adds that he is a big believer in the power of what he terms "impromptu mentoring"—those unpredictable moments in business and in life when you observe a success principle in action and integrate it into your own belief system. Indeed, *A Message from Garcia* is rich with examples of people he has worked with, met, or just heard about who made a profound impact on his life. Here are a few examples of these men and women and the lessons Garcia gleaned from them:

Write down your life's dreams.
Garcia shares the amazing story of **Charles D. Kelman**, ophthalmic physician and eye surgeon, professional musician, inventor with more than 150 patents to his name, and winner of numerous awards. How did Kelman achieve such astonishing success, and, more to the point, happiness? One of the keys was a 28-page book (author unknown) titled simply *It Works*. This little book explains the critical importance of writing down your life's dreams, reviewing them at least three times a day, and discussing them with no one. Garcia has brought this simple yet powerful idea to the Internet Age with his Web-based software program Success Compass™—www.successcompass.com—which helps you identify your dreams and goals and then sends you an e-mail reminder three times a day.

Treat everyone you meet as if he or she were a war hero.
When Garcia was a cadet at the Air Force Academy, he knew a squadron janitor named **William Crawford**. To some cadets, this man who scrubbed toilets and mopped floors was a nonentity; to others he was an object of ridicule. Then, one day a cadet discovered that during World War II the lowly janitor had been a war hero, saving lives, getting captured by German soldiers and ending up as a P.O.W. He was a Medal of Honor winner! Mr. Crawford told the cadet that after he retired as a master sergeant from the Army in 1967, he took the janitor's spot so he could teach future Air Force officers what he had learned from his experiences in the military. "I keep a large painting of Mr. Crawford in my office to remind me that within everyone is the potential to be a hero," writes Garcia. "Not every person you meet will be a war hero. But if you want to be successful, treat everyone you meet with respect."

Pursue your passion, regardless of the cost.

To fulfill her family's wishes, **Theresa Park** attended Harvard Law School. For 15 months after she graduated, she worked as a high-powered corporate lawyer. But she felt unfulfilled. Feeling drawn to a career in publishing, she moved to New York City and looked for work as a literary agent. Finally, she found a job as an assistant to two agents. The salary was only $18,000 a year, less than half of what her former secretary made! But Park stuck with it, working hard all day and combing the "slush pile" (a term for rejected manuscripts) at night. After about a year, she came upon a manuscript about two elderly people in love. Touched and impressed, she contacted the aspiring author, a 28-year-old pharmaceutical salesman. Pitching the manuscript as the next *Bridges of Madison County*, Park worked to sell it to different publishing houses. Jamie Rabb at Warner Brothers finally bit, with an offer of $500,000. But, unbelievably, the agent said no. She was looking for a seven-figure deal! Ten minutes later, Rabb called back, offering $1 million! The deal was done. The author? Nicholas Sparks. The novel? *The Notebook*, which spent over two years on bestseller lists around the world. Park is now one of the most sought-after literary agents in the business.

Bring at least three solutions to the table.

After graduating from the U.S. Air Force Academy, Garcia became special assistant to **General John R. Galvin** who later was named Supreme Allied Commander of NATO. When the General gave Garcia his first assignment, Garcia nervously came back with a list of questions. That's when General Galvin gave him some valuable advice: "Don't bring me problems; bring me solutions." Later, after Garcia came back with a solution, the General clarified further: "If you always think of at least three different ways to solve a problem, you will look at things from a different perspective and you'll make sure that you are not grasping at the first solution that comes to mind."

Work hard & play hard.

When he served as a White House Fellow, Garcia worked as a Special Assistant to former Secretary of Education and Drug Czar **William Bennett**. He writes: "When Bill Bennett was the Drug Czar, he shunned the Washington social scene in favor of a more reserved personal life. But it wasn't all work and no play for Bennett. Most Sundays a group of us would play a spirited game of touch football with Bennett . . . [He] looked at sports as a metaphor for life and he believed that sports are a way to learn, after either victory or defeat, that another day, another chance, comes tomorrow. And sports are a good way to put work behind you for a little while."

If you can learn a valuable life lesson from anyone, then he or she qualifies as an impromptu mentor, says Garcia. Looked at in this way, mentoring isn't something you benefit from only at work, or something you outgrow. And it most definitely isn't a one-way street: Garcia firmly believes in returning the favor and teaching others what you, yourself, have learned about the nature of success.

"Not only my career, but also my life philosophy, has been shaped by watching and learning from some of the most fascinating people in the world," says Garcia. "I am grateful for that, and I want to return the favor. That's why I currently mentor several young people through my work at Sterling Financial, and it's also why I wrote my book. My advice is this: look for mentors everywhere, and *be* a mentor every chance you get. Yes, it's a big part of the new business ethic. But more to the point, it's a major key to success in every area of life."

# # #

About the Author:

Charles Patrick Garcia, 42, is a graduate of the U.S. Air Force Academy, a highly decorated military officer, a Columbia Law School graduate and a former White House Fellow. In 1997, at the age of thirty-six, he founded Sterling Financial Group of Companies with three people, which has grown to more than sixty offices in seven countries. The company was named the number one fastest-growing Hispanic-owned business in the country by *Hispanic Business* magazine and number eight on the Inc 500 list of fastest-growing privately-held companies in the nation. For his success across many fields, Garcia was named one of the nation's 100 most influential Hispanics, and his leadership abilities have earned him a role in the administration of three U.S. Presidents, a Cabinet Secretary, a Governor and a former NATO Supreme Allied Commander. Garcia has received the Key to the City of Panama, and President Mireya Moscoso honored him for his success as a Panamanian-American in the United States. *Hispanic Today* magazine featured him in a cover-story, "Committing to Hispanic America," and *Univision* television featured him in their series "Orgullo Hispano," spotlighting him as a Hispanic who has made "an exceptional impact on the culture and life of American society." The book's success has triggered numerous media appearances and coverage in print, radio, and both English and Spanish language national and international television. Garcia's provocative commentary on significant issues of national concern have been sought by CROSSFIRE, FOX News, CNN, CBS, Univision, Telemundo, and CNN en Español. During the War in Iraq, Garcia served as Telemundo's military analyst, providing daily live-behind-the-desk commentary.

About the Book:

A Message from Garcia: Yes, You Can Succeed (2003, John Wiley & Sons, ISBN: 0-471-44893-1, $24.95) is available at your local bookstore or by calling 1-800-225-5945. In Canada, call 1-800-567-4797.

69. A PR agency's contacts won't help you if your book does not contain some newsworthy ideas or tips.

Publishers or authors may seek to hire a PR agency or publicist on the basis of their contacts. It's a myth, however, that the contacts alone are going to get you and your book on national television. Producers and hosts are not going to let a publicist talk them into putting someone on a show whose book does not highlight newsworthy material worth the air time or who, in any way, shape or form, is not going to perform well as a guest. Contacts do count, yes, but the publicist's ability to write a great press release, guide the production of a great video, or groom you for a brilliant appearance as a guest are all more important. With an eye for connecting your message to breaking news, a good publicist will find the merchandisable stories in what you have written and call them to the attention of a broad range of media, both print and broadcast, to enhance your visibility and the demand for your book.

70. Controversy sells books.

Avoid "PR Prozac," which lulls readers to sleep. Get the hard angles. What a publicist hopes to find is "breaking news," information or insights so revolutionary that your book becomes not a feature story but a news flash. If your how-to can effectively challenge conventional wisdom in a field, you will get a much higher, and longer, ride in the media. Strongly opinionated material stands out in a crowded marketplace.

71. You can get endorsements from best-selling authors, even if you do not know them personally.

Some of them have a policy of endorsing whatever appealing books are presented to them because the book cover provides an "ad" for them and their latest work. Some you approach may turn you down, of course, but be persistent. If you solicit endorsements from enough authors whose work has some relation to yours, you will probably land two or three "yeses."

In one case, a client author of Rocks-DeHart sent his manuscript and a cover letter to a household-name Hollywood figure, pointing out the connection between his book and the celebrity's interests. The celebrity responded with lightning speed—and an *endorsement!* You can ALWAYS reach authors by addressing a letter to them c/o their publisher. In some cases, with a little research, you can locate the authors' home or office address. A number of best-selling authors now have their contact info printed on a back page of their books or on their websites.

72. Titles are not under copyright.

You heard correctly: someone else can put exactly the same title on a book as you put on a book you published last year—and you cannot sue them. To protect their titles, some authors have gone to the very expensive length of trademarking them. *Chicken Soup for the Soul*® is an example.

73. When a newspaper or magazine runs a story on you or your book, don't think you can willy-nilly run off 500 copies and start sending them out.

That story, typically, will be under copyright. The publication will likely expect you to *purchase* reprints. These may run anywhere from $150 to $2,000 for, say, 2,000 copies. One benefit: if there was a mistake made anywhere in the story, such as the misspelling of your name (which actually happened to Celia), the publication can fix the mistake before it runs off the reprint. Sometimes you also can add your company logo and contact information to the article when you purchase a reprint. Always ask for electronic rights as part of the reprint purchase. Reprints are great for consultants' or speakers' kits. One caveat: Be careful about including badly outdated articles in your kit.

This may vary according to the subject and the prominence of the publication that ran your article or interview. As a rule, however, more than two years old is probably too old.

74. Authors need to be conscientious and energetic about building their "platforms."

Market not just your book but your whole program, whether it be consulting, motivational speaking, holding workshops or whatever. A platform, typically, is built by a combination of events or appearances, supported by a mix of public relations and advertising. Book signings (especially the kind where you do a talk and answer questions, possibly using handouts or video projection), radio and television appearances, interviews or feature stories on you and your message in newspapers and magazines (the more the better) . . . all of these work together for platform building.

75. A platform, once built, must constantly be nurtured.

Be careful what you wish for: Once you have achieved a high-profile reputation, keeping it burnished will require money, time and energy. Many of our clients bill by the day and are on a plane some 150 days of the year. That can be both profitable and lonely. So be sure to ask yourself: Is that a lifestyle that works for me?

76. Advertise to the trade.

ForeWord magazine, the leading journal in independent publishing, has wonderful cameo ads in four color for $225. Ingram has catalog-magazines such as *Advance, Body Mind & Spirit, Home & Hearth*. Baker & Taylor too has a magazine. Then there are such important trade publications as *Publisher's Weekly, Library Journal* and *Kirkus Reviews*. Advertisements placed in such periodicals will definitely put your book covers and publication data in front of trade bookstore buyers and librarians. R.R. Bowker Company offers to make your sell sheets or other small circulars "ride-alongs" with their main annual catalog in a mailing to 3,200 bookstores, and also include your title in "best-bet" collections of books, niche by niche, on their website. Being publicists, we prefer editorial coverage to advertising for a number of reasons, but do think of book marketing as an ongoing trial and error project utilizing many platforms for exposure.

77. Vanity presses are barred from many major bookstores.

Your dream of being a published author may incline you to cast your lot with any number of vanity publishers operating regionally or nationally. Be careful: If a publisher is willing to do little more than run spell check and then set in book type whatever you send, print 3,000 copies and bind it in soft or hard cover, ship you the books and an invoice, you are probably dealing with a vanity publisher. The more demanding a subsidy publisher is of the final editorial product and the graphic packaging of your book, the less likely it is that you are in the hands of a sheer vanity press. Subsidy publishers come in many shades and stripes. The best of them will turn your business down flat if in their judgment you do not, even with their critical suggestions and editing, have any prospect of making your manuscript into a publishable book. Major bookstores keep a list of vanity publishers, and in most cases, will bar those books from ever showing up on their shelves. Some of the small bookstores may put up less of a fuss. But the bottom line is, just because you can pay someone to publish your book, doesn't mean the book will have any benefit or sales once it is published.

78. Always carry a copy of your book with you—or at least advertise it on your business card.

If this tip seems out of place in the "marketing" section, that just means you're under the misconception that marketing has to be complicated. It doesn't. Sometimes handing a copy of your book to the right person at the right time can be the ultimate marketing move! So always have a copy with you—in your briefcase or purse or in the trunk of your car. If you run into an important editor or a potential client, you can hand them an autographed copy and make an immediate connection.

If this advice seems impractical, there is another option: have a picture of the cover of your book printed on your business card. Since technology has taken over, giving out a colorful business card is actually a unique marketing tool. Not only will this serve as a constant reminder that your book exists, it will make your card stand out from the crowd . . . and who knows where *that* might lead?

VII. S A L E S

79. Enthusiasm is the driving force in book sales.

That enthusiasm needs to begin with the author, who should inject it into the tone of his or her book. The wave of enthusiasm needs to be picked up by the publisher and then should wash out onto the world of wholesale and retail book buying, all the way to the individual consumer. In other words, if you've got some great ideas, be excited about them and about your goal of reaching a large public.

80. Publishing happens by season.

And the main seasons are "Spring" and "Fall." More recently some publishers have instituted a "Summer" season. There is no "Winter." A "Spring" book might be published anywhere from December of the previous year through May. "Fall" books start in August and run through

November. If a publisher does abide by a "Summer" season, those books will probably be published in May, June and July. "Spring" will stop with April and "Fall" will begin with August. The seasons are captured in catalogs, sent well in advance of the publication of the books therein to 3,000 or more booksellers nationwide.

81. Large bookstores actually sell display space up front.

One of several reasons large publishers are advantaged in the book-selling game is that they rent premium display space for their titles. Thus a table of "New Releases" close to the register in many bookstores will be reserved for books whose publishers have forked out money to the stores to grab those spaces. Smaller publishers and most self-publishers cannot compete for this space and thus see their books relegated to less desirable shelves farther back, where, in most cases, their titles will be displayed only "spine out" (not front cover out). So if you self publish or have your book put out by a small press, think of other ways to compete. Bring a well-designed poster to the store several days ahead of your book signing, for instance. They may well be happy to put it up and thus feature your book and pave the way for your appearance.

82. Books that are effectively self-published are indeed a way of getting the attention of a major publisher.

What they will look at hardest, however, is not the book itself but its sales trajectory. Selling even 1,000 copies of a book in a restricted local area may tell a publisher with a good distribution system that they can project sales of 10,000 or more nationally (if the book has genuine national appeal).

83. You cannot make a book take off simply by throwing money at it.

Buying your own books back from stores, for instance, will most likely NOT help you achieve the *New York Times* bestseller list. That list is compiled from sales from a selected number of bookstores nationwide. Unless you had insider information and access to the *Times'* list of stores (which may, in any case, change from month to month), you would have no idea where to buy your books.

You can indeed buy books—or have friends or associates do it—from Amazon.com and make your book move up the ranks. The Amazon.com ranking of a book is a number that booksellers may notice—especially if you can get your book down below 1,000 in overall sales rank.

84. Have a good elevator speech about your book.

You know, 45 seconds to a minute, a concise pitch that zeros in on benefits to readers. It should answer the question: Why bother to read this book? WIIFM??? ("What's In It for Me?") Often, the best line of your "elevator speech" is the line that should lead off the blurb on your back cover, or be set off in that little pond of white space next to your book's description in the publisher's catalog. You never know who you'll run into in an elevator—or at a meeting. It just may be a woman who heads up marketing for a conglomerate whose employees or customers could benefit from reading your book. Or the manager of a regional chain of bookstores.

85. Seven out of ten self-published books do not make the cut at Barnes & Noble.

What the small press department at B & N sees too much of includes: weak or amateurish covers or interior design, poor printing and/or binding, overpriced books, books that did not merit any reviews or were never properly submitted for reviews and books that are not supported by a dynamic marketing plan.

86. It's all about "sell-through."

That means that when your book is put into stores, it sells out and has to be reordered. Having this happen time and again creates an impression in the stores that the book is a winner. It "sells through." Books that do NOT sell through get returned for credit against other books from the same distribution group or even for cash. Publishing is one industry where a sale is not a sale until a consumer plunks down cash or plastic for your book and takes it home. Then and only then can you consider your book "bought and paid for." When working on your balance sheet, your "return reserve" fund could have a significant impact on your bottom line! Some return reserves run as much as 20 percent! To get your store sales started right, it's important that a good opening wave of publicity about your book hit the media as your book arrives on the shelves. We've also heard of publishers who ship a smaller quantity than ordered in an attempt to avoid returns.

87. In today's publishing merry-go-round, small publishers (or self publishers) should aim to generate two-thirds of their revenue from "nontraditional sales," and only one-third from trade bookstore sales.

This is a tough one. Reality dictates, however, that those who wish to survive, or even thrive, in publishing below the level of the behemoth houses in New York and San Francisco, bear down energetically on the many avenues of sales for their titles outside general trade. These include online services such as Amazon.com, BN.com, Bookazine, direct mail and website sales, bulk sales to companies and organizations, premium sales to companies that may want to send out your book with a compatible product (a book on backyard barbeque cooking with a gas grill, for example) and "back-of-the-room" sales after a talk or a workshop. Nontraditional sales also includes outlets that are not strictly bookstores—such as Target, Wal-Mart, Best Buy, pharmacy and supermarket chains, gift shops and state parks.

One of the best ways of achieving nontraditional sales is by building databases of individuals and organizations in your market niche. If you're writing about sales, collect names and e-mails of salespeople; if you're writing about sailing, same goes with yachtsmen and weekend pleasure sailcraft owners. And so on. Celia was able to sell a substantial amount of copies of *Organizing the Good Life* to a business mentoring/coaching group in Canada even before the book was published. Once you get the hang of pre-pub sales, you'll find it a lot easier—and not intimidating as a concept.

Let's run through the revenue on a $20 retail list title. One-third of sales of 3,500 through trade bookstores equals

1,166 copies at 50 percent (or $10): $11,660. Two-thirds of revenue from nontraditional sources at an average of two-thirds of retail list price, or 2,333 copies at $13.20 each comes to $30,799, for a combined trade and non-trade sales of $42,459. Author's royalties would vary, according to how many books the author sold personally. Normally, publishers allow authors to buy books for resale at a 40 percent discount; the authors may then sell the books either at full retail list or at a discount of their choosing.

88. Effective distribution of books to the trade is key to success.

The distribution process is crucial to success, and a thorough analysis of which distributor is best suited for your needs is a required step.

When distribution goes smoothly, publishers can be very happy. Unfortunately, in recent years there have been glitches in the distribution process, and numerous small publishers (and self publishers) have been hurt—some beyond their capacity to recover. Distributors have gone broke—with disastrous consequences for a number of publishers. Make sure you fully understand your contract with your distributor so you are not at the mercy of any financial problems they may encounter.

89. Send free samples to selected bookstores, but remember to stamp "sample" on the page edges.

Large, in red letters. That way stores will not be able to return those sample copies to Ingram for credit. Sample copies are, however, a good idea and may be your best bet for getting independent stores to order your book. Include a flier with ordering information.

90. Only 300 or so people in the entire United States reportedly earn a complete living by writing books.

That means that the overwhelming majority of authors must rely on speaking, consulting, workshops, seminars, teaching, research, or another income avenue in the public or private sector for the lion's share of their income.

91. E-books have not made it—at least not in general trade book selling.

A best-selling trade (general reading) e-book these days is one that has sold 67 copies! For technical material it may be another matter. Many technical people like the idea of being able to call up a file on their computer screen to check a process or to review data.

92. Hold back on doing an audio book.

You should first assure that the regular printed book is selling well. A rule of thumb: wait until the printed book has sold 10,000 copies before doing an audio version. Generally, audio books will sell only about one-fifth as many copies as the printed book.

Exception to the rule: If your subject is one that people need to train in, companies buying the work in bulk may like the idea of giving their people a chance to listen to the material during their morning commute. Another idea is to take one important subject in your book and create a CD on that specific niche subject. Here's an example: one of our clients, Maribeth Kuzmeski, wrote *Red Zone Marketing*. One of our favorite parts of her book (and the media's favorite part) is what she calls "Creating a Client Experience." After the book was published, she produced a Client Experience CD, which takes listeners in-depth on the subject. Not only did she expand (and not just duplicate) her product line, she "zoned in" on a hot topic her readers would enjoy.

93.

Book tours are expensive and rarely make back their costs in books sold during signings. Nonetheless, book tours are an excellent idea if done in the right spirit.

The average number of books sold at a trade bookstore signing is four. Thus, as can easily be grasped, it is difficult to generate the kind of income from such sales that will offset air travel, lodgings and meals on the road. Build your tour to coincide with your regularly scheduled business and vacation travel, however, and you have a winner. Just be sure you combine broadcast and print interviews with signings.

It's ideal to have your signing announced in the local press two or three days beforehand, and on the day of too, if possible, and have yourself on local radio or TV the day before or the morning of the event. This, of course, probably requires the help of professional publicists to be done "right."

94.

Be savvy about lead time for booking signings. And media.

The large chain bookstores—and the large independents, too—have monthly newsletters. You definitely want your signing announced in the newsletter of any store where you will appear. Thus the signing must typically be booked six to eight weeks in advance. TV talk shows, even local editions, are often booked two to three months in advance. National shows may book anywhere from three to six months in advance. Local radio and print interviews usually can be booked two weeks in advance. For national radio shows, figure at least six weeks.

95. "Buzz" sells books.

We're talking here about the "noise" you make among prospective readers *before* the book is issued. Databases of professionals or others in the niche you are targeting can be gold if you can get the right prepublication announcements into the right hands. This can be done by postcards, fliers, faxes, e-mail, or sales letters sent by snail mail. It is especially helpful to let experts in the field see and comment upon your book before it appears in the stores. Excerpts of your book published in magazines or newsletters ahead of your "pub date" will help the cause immensely. Word of mouth is still the most powerful form of advertising, so make sure the news about your book's powerful content starts moving along the grapevine. Create a master VIP list and make sure everyone on it is informed about your book.

96. Acknowledgments and thank yous will take you far.

The acknowledgment section of a book gives you a five-star opportunity to thank the many people who have helped you achieve publication, including clients, coworkers, friends and family. Everyone whose name you list is potentially an extra hand on your sales force. Editors and literary agents will appreciate a mention, but so will graphic artists and other production people—and maybe even the clients you've worked with who have impacted your expertise and knowledge. And while we're on gratitude, remember to send a thank-you note to each bookstore that invites you for a signing and each radio or TV talk show that has you as a guest. Tasteful notes and complimentary signed copies of your book should become the norm.

97. Media training makes a difference.

If you don't spend time, and perhaps some money, on media training, you'll be less effective, especially on TV. Media training can range from a few sessions to a complete course, costing anywhere from $1,000 up to $5,000 or more. There was an instance where the president of a company that made parachutes for escaping tall buildings was live on a national morning TV show along with an aide who completely bungled his demonstration of how to strap on a parachute in an emergency. Either that should have been rehearsed so well he could have done it quickly and correctly, or they should have used a video clip for that segment. But the company president's appearance was a complete disaster because of how clumsy the aide was with the demonstration. A good rule: Don't ever attempt to do anything on TV where you don't know what the outcome will be before you start.

Clothes, too, can count big. Celia recalls the time when she went on a PBS program wearing a brand new turtleneck sweater she had bought for the occasion. Appearing on the same show was a woman in a loose-fitting v-necked blue shirt that Celia thought looked a bit shopworn. On TV, however, the turtleneck made Celia's face seem puffed up, whereas the woman with the old blue shirt looked just fine. Sometimes you can avoid a clothing *faux pas* by asking your publicist or the producer specific questions regarding dress and appearance.

98. Make sure distributors and wholesalers are informed of all reviews, advertising and media exposure for your book.

More than one sadder-but-wiser author has found herself on a book tour featuring TV, radio and newspaper coverage, only to discover when she arrived at a store for a signing that none of her books had arrived from a wholesaler's warehouse. Media exposure that occurs when your books aren't available in the stores is a tremendous waste. The reason stores don't have books on hand in such instances probably is due to a breakdown of the vital communication that must occur between a publisher and the book trade outlets (distributor, wholesaler, bookstore). Not only must media be set up to promote a book, word of impending media exposure must be conveyed to the right people to trigger a flow of books to stores in areas affected by such exposure. Processing and shipping time must be taken into account. Ten-day advance notice usually will suffice, and sometimes books can be expedited from warehouse to stores in 72 hours or less—but don't count on it. We always recommend that an author travel with at least 10 books with her.

99. Don't be a stranger to your local library; while there, be sure to familiarize yourself with the LMP (The Literary Marketplace).

Fondly referred to in publishing circles as "The LMP," this two-volume reference annual packages up virtually everything you need to know about who's who and who does what in North American publishing. The volumes were acquired from R.R. Bowker Company in the year 2000 by Information Today, 143 Old Marleton Pike, Medford, NJ, 08055-8750, www.literarymarketplace.com. Volume I gives contact information and publishing proclivities of North American publishers, literary agents and editorial services freelancers and companies. It also provides a calendar of events in the publishing world, information on publishing and writing courses, seminars and workshops and on literary and other publishing prizes. Comprehensive yellow pages sections give alphabetical listings for first organizations, then individuals in publishing. Volume II furnishes information on public relations agencies and solo practitioners that specialize in book promotion, book reviewers, translators, art services, prepress (typesetting and design) services, publishing consultants, book packagers, stock photo agencies and photographers, newspaper columnists, TV and radio shows that feature books and authors and news services and feature syndicates. In other words, between the two volumes you have a not-to-be-missed wealth of information to help the cause of developing your book, finding an agent or publisher or hiring the right people to help you self-publish, and also boost the cause of launching and promoting your book.

A separate publication is *The International Literary Marketplace*. As the name indicates, this is a similar annual that focuses on publishers, agents and others associated with book publishing who work in countries other than the USA and Canada.

100. Get a copy of Kirsch's Guide to the Book Contract

Published by Acrobat Books (Los Angeles), this is a must-read, keep-handy book for authors, publishers and agents. Book contracts vary tremendously from publisher to publisher. Typically, contracts heavily favor publishers' rights. Agents and attorneys who specialize in intellectual property are almost always able to tip the scales and secure a better deal for authors than the authors could negotiate on their own.

Jonathan Kirsch is a partner in the Los Angeles firm Kirsch & Mitchell, specialists in intellectual property matters and publishing law. The issues he deals with in his guide are complex and daunting, but you will serve your interests well by diving in and learning what's what, clause by clause, in a book contract.

101. Our final tip: Don't delude yourself into thinking this book has taught you everything you need to know.

Yes, we have worked hard to bring you valuable, up-to-date insights into the challenging world of how-to book publishing. Indeed, we hope that the 101 tips plus the additional articles on pitching to the media and working with wholesalers and distributors will spare you incalculable pain and grief. (And such turmoil has indeed resulted for countless authors and self publishers who ploughed into the dark night of book publishing without most of the information contained in this book.) That said, there is *always* more to learn, and not merely trivia but vital techniques and poignant realities.

To keep learning, it's a good idea to join one or more trade associations in publishing. The most prominent of these for independent publishers is Publishers Marketing Association, 627 Aviation Way, Manhattan Beach, California, 90266, Jan Nathan, executive director. Second in line is the Small Publishers Association of North America (SPAN), P.O. Box 1306, Buena Vista, Colorado, 81211-1306. Belonging to one or both of these associations will bring you their tip-packed newsletters and discounts to subscribe to publishing journals, to send books with certain freight carriers and to attend seminars and workshops. Also consider subscribing to one or more publishing journals. *Publishers Weekly* and *ForeWord Magazine* are two of the more prominent journals. *Publishers Lunch* is an online newsletter issued on virtually a daily basis by Michael Cader, a successful New York-based book packager. It is free for the asking. To sign up, dial up www.publisherslunch.com. And please delve into other books on publishing. We especially like John Kremer's *1001 Ways to Market Your Books*, Tom Woll's *Publishing for Profit*, Marilyn and Tom Ross's book *The Complete Guide to Self Publishing* and Judith Appelbaum's classic text *How to Get Happily Published*. Publishing courses, seminars and workshops on publishing abound. The PMA University, always scheduled to run just before Book Expo America (BEA), the leading national trade show in publishing, delivers powerful value for your enrollment money. We recommend going to the BEA, which is usually held in May or June. Even if you make only one new contact or pick up one great idea, it is worth it! We hope to see you there!

20 Do's and Don'ts for Landing the Big Media Hits

DO put together the best media list possible for your story. Be sure to include print (magazines and newspapers), broadcast (radio and TV) and Internet media. Make careful editor selection for each media venue.

DO think of all the possible pitching angles for your story. Make sure you take the time to match the appropriate angle to each media outlet on your list. Become familiar with the media you are pitching.

DO practice your pitch. Call and leave it on your own voice mail to see how it sounds. Have friends critique it.

DO get started right now. Just do it! Don't wait until all the planets are aligned to start pitching. You can always find

1,000 other things to do, but make yourself get started. Set a realistic goal and stick to it. Commit to 50 calls a day or whatever your schedule will allow. But remember, if you have truly done your homework, each new pitch should become easier and easier.

DO begin pitching the smaller media outlets first. It will give you a chance to refine your pitch before you move on to the bigger outlets. But don't spend too much time there. As Elaine Biech says in *The Business of Consulting*, go for the big fish. You will spend just as much time baiting the hook.

DO ask if now is a good time to pitch a story. Editors and producers appreciate this courtesy so much that if it *isn't* a good time, they will usually tell you when to call back. Also, be aware of any breaking news the day you are pitching so that you don't call at the worst possible time and embarrass yourself.

DO think logically about the best times to call. Typically, Monday mornings and Friday afternoons are hectic for everyone, including the media. Late afternoons are often bad for reporters at dailies because of deadlines. The days immediately following a holiday are often bad as well, as reporters are playing catch up.

DO anticipate reaching lots of voice mail. This means you have to keep your pitch concise and to the point as you leave an effective voice mail regarding the press kit and book they should have received.

DON'T ignore editor preferences. If an editor's voice mail says she prefers fax or e-mail, use that avenue to pitch your story.

DON'T ever be rude to the media. Treat all media with courtesy, no matter how important or unimportant you deem them to be or how they treat you. Never, ever burn bridges, even if you think you are right. It is a very small world.

DON'T let rejections discourage you, but do let them guide you. If you are striking out in one market, move to another. Remember, you may have to kiss a lot of frogs before you find a prince.

DON'T forget to leave your phone number at least twice in the message. Always leave it at the beginning of the message and again at the end. That way, if the editor misses your number the first time, she doesn't have to listen to the whole message again.

DO recite your phone number very slowly. Pretend you are writing it in the air with your finger and learn to use that pace when leaving your message.

DO invest in voice mail. It is inexpensive and it's much more reliable and professional than an answering machine.

DON'T be rigid with your pitching. You don't have to exhaust your media list to decide your pitch may not be working. Be flexible, and if you see no one is biting, rethink it and refine it.

DON'T call editors just to ask if they received your materials. Find a way to make each call worthwhile. This is best done with a slight variation of the pitch in the press materials or a reason that compels them to look for your press release after they get your call.

DO engage in practices that make it easy for the media to work with you. Return calls promptly and send all materials immediately. If a media person requests your book, send it right away, along with the press release and a personalized note reminding her of your call. Do this even if she already has your release! Include your contact info (phone number and e-mail) in several places so it is easy for her to get in touch with you.

DO keep meticulous notes on what people tell you. These will be invaluable in learning individual preferences, following up and strategizing your next move.

DON'T forget the importance of a follow-up call. Again, don't call just to make sure they got the book! Use the call as your opportunity to provide editors with additional information that will (hopefully) compel them to act.

DO be persistent, but not pushy. There are lots of ways to keep your information in front of the media without annoying them.

Glossary of Publishing Terms

Acquisition editor—The person at a publishing company who reviews and rates incoming manuscripts for possible publication and then supervises the publication process.

Advance—A sum paid to the author in anticipation of royalty earnings.

Back matter—Traditionally considered "appendices." Whatever follows the last page of the last chapter. Among elements found in back matter are: bibliography, "resource section" (including videotapes, audiotapes, websites, addresses of relevant organizations), technical, legal, or other documents germane to the book but too long or unwieldy to have included in the main text, an index, biographical sketch of the author, notes on type, composition, or printing.

Barcode—EAN barcodes are essential for any book to be sold in major bookstores, chains and independents. A book's ISBN number and its price are typically run on the upper edges of the scanner readable barcode. There are software programs available to generate one's own barcode, but let your printer help you with this.

Bowker—The R.R. Bowker Company holds the authority to issue ISBN numbers and is, in many ways, a pivotal entity in the book industry. Bowker is the publisher of the Literary Marketplace (LMP), the main annual reference works on who is doing what in publishing, both U.S. and foreign. Bowker also provides a number of important advertising services to help publishers promote their new titles "to the trade."

Casebound—Binding for hardbound books. Also designated as "cloth."

Cataloging-in-Publication (CIP)—A publisher must have a minimum of five books published under a set of ISBN numbers before this number will be granted for a book by the Library of Congress. It is used in cross referencing and inter-library searches. The CIP program helps prepare prepublication cataloging records. It is intended for books likely to be acquired widely by American libraries. Books paid for or subsidized by individual authors or books published by a house that publishes the works of only one or two authors are ineligible for the CIP program. However, these titles may be eligible for the Electronic Preassigned Control Number (EPCN) program. Visit http://pcn.loc.gov/pcn for more information on the EPCN program.

Co-op publishing—An arrangement of cost sharing between an author and a publisher, and corresponding division of net proceeds from sales of a book. Percentage of cost sharing may split in any number of ways—50/50, 60/40, 70/30 or whatever the two parties agree upon. In an unstable economy, it is becoming more and more popular.

Colophon—The way a publisher prints its name on the title page (and sometimes back flap, back cover and/or spine). May include a graphic symbol (such as a pine tree, a mountain top, a detail of a printing press) along with the letters spelling out the publisher's name. Normally, a colophon should be trademarked.

Copy editor—Person who corrects grammar and spelling in a manuscript and checks facts for accuracy and conformity.

Copyright—First usage today is considered protection for editorial or graphic material. Printing the symbol © or the word "copyright" followed by a name of holder of rights (usually the author(s) or the publisher) consolidates and reinforces the rights. Registration of copyright is accomplished by filling out and sending in the appropriate forms to the Library of Congress.

Copyright page—This page is almost always printed on the verso (flip) side of the title page. It will contain the copyright information, ISBN number, Library of Congress number, Cataloging-in-Publication data, name of publisher and often the publisher's contact information (address, email, website, fax) and credits (such as cover design, editorial coordination, etc.) for persons other than the author who worked on the book.

It also may include permission to reprint previously published material, a printing history of the work, country in which the work was printed, a key to illustrations and information about special discounts for bulk sales.

E-book—A book published in electronic form that can be downloaded to computers or handheld devices.

Front matter—Pages from half-title page to the page before the beginning of the first chapter. This section typically includes some or all of the following: half-title page, title page, copyright page, dedication page, acknowledgments, table of contents, foreword and introduction. There is no set-in-stone order for elements in front matter, except that the foreword should always precede the introduction. Roman numerals frequently are used as page numbers for front matter. Arabic numerals are normally used from the first page of Chapter One all the way through the end of the book (including "back matter").

Galleys—A term for what are actually "page proofs." Publicists use them to reach long-lead magazines and industry trade magazines prior to the actual book's being published.

Ghostwriter—A writer or co-writer who is not credited on the work.

Gutter—Downsloping area formed by the inside margins of pages in a book. It is important to assure that these margins are generous enough to prevent readers from having to "read into the gutter."

Half-title page—When one is used, the first page of the book. Printed here is just the book's title (not the subtitle and not the author's name), usually about one-third of a page down from the top and often centered. A half-title page gives a book an elegant opening.

Imprint—A publishing name used by a publisher on the title page, back cover and/or spine of a book. The imprint may be the actual name of the company or another name. In today's mega-merger world, many fine old publishing names have become "imprints" of conglomerates: Scribner is an imprint of Simon&Schuster; Times Books, launched decades ago by *The New York Times*, is an imprint of Random House. New imprints appear all the time, while older ones disappear.

ISBN number—Stands for "International Standard Book Number." Issued by R.R. Bowker Company. Every book needs one so it can be identified correctly.

Library of Congress number—Number for an individual book issued by the Library of Congress. This will be the catalog number for the book when it resides on the shelves of the Library of Congress.

Line editor—See copy editor

Marketing plan—Comprehensive plan for the launch and early promotion of a book. It normally includes where prepublication and post-publication review copies will be sent, in what venues the book will be announced and/or advertised, what media outlets will be solicited for stories on the book's major themes or interviews with the author and where book signings will be set up. If you are a speaker or consultant, it should also include how you will use the book to grow your business (i.e., get the word out).

Media hits—Print or broadcast outlets that respond with a "yes" when solicited to do a review, article, author interview or other feature on a new book. The term also is used to designate actual published reviews or articles or broadcast programs done live or else taped and aired. Stay organized so that media hits can be effectively merchandised to your publisher, distributor, clients and speakers bureaus.

Media kit—Same as "press kit," though perhaps tailored more for broadcast media.

Page proofs —Printed pages, unbound, sent by the printer to the publisher for final corrections before the book is printed.

Perfectbound—Binding for softbound books ("paperbacks").

Press kit—Usually encased in a 9 x 12 presentation folder with pockets. Should contain a cover letter (personalized to each media outlet), one or more news releases on most catchy or newsworthy elements of a book, interview questions (often with responses), best recent clips of published articles or interviews. Be careful not to cram too many elements into a press kit. Up to five or six attractive sheets are okay.

Press release—The actual information you want the media to write about is typically contained in these two to three sheets of paper.

Print on Demand (P.O.D.)—A laser-printing technology that makes it cost effective to print books in small quantities (from a few dozen to around 400). It now takes an expert to tell the difference in quality of printing between web press and P.O.D. (in most cases). P.O.D. has made possible an explosion of books from new authors under such subsidy imprints as iUniverse, lst Books and Tandey. Traditional publishers use P.O.D. to test market new books, to customize books (for instance, different forewords and endorsements according to different distribution sectors) and to keep backlist titles in print when it would be inefficient to run 1,000 or less copies on a web press.

Proposal—The major instrument for conveying the essentials of nonfiction book manuscript. (See p.19).

Pub data—Salient information on a book for purposes of distribution and sales: Title, subtitle, author, publisher, month and year of expected release, ISBN number, number of pages, type of binding, retail list price. Key for sell sheets, catalogs, booksellers and wholesalers databases.

Pub date—Date a publisher conveys to the bookselling industry for the expected availability of a new title. Books are often released ahead of the publication date (by two to six weeks). Releasing a book after the pub date is considered bad form and may hurt a publisher's reputation in the trade.

Query—A letter to a publisher or agent proposing a manuscript or book proposal for review. Query letters should be short (1 to 3 pages). They should include: the central theme of the book, notes on the projected readership, status of the work (how much is ready for inspection), author's publishing and professional credits and bio sketch, notes on author's marketing plan. A good query letter should sum up, very concisely, the elements of a book proposal and leave an impression that a good strong proposal is available for review upon request.

Remainders—Books removed from bookstore circulation and sold at steep discounts to "Remainder Houses," who will sell them back to bookstores to be featured as discounted books. A book that began retailing for $20 might be sold to a remainder house for $1-$2, then reappear on bookstore shelves as a book "discounted to $6."

Returns—Books sent back to wholesalers by bookstores as "unsold." (Books often are sent back after four to six months, occasionally even sooner.) Wholesaler may then return books to publishers. In the book trade, in effect, every book is actually "on consignment;" even though monies may be paid for a sale, they can be claimed back if the book does not "sell through." A book is not truly "sold" until a consumer pays for it at a store and takes it home. Returns are the bane of the publishing industry. There has been much discussion but thus far no resolution of this thorny problem.

Review copies—Book copies sent out to magazines, journals, newspapers and other periodicals. A certain number of such publications will accept ONLY pre-publication copies, commonly known as "bound galleys" (even though they are no longer "galleys" but actually page proofs). The majority of publications that review books will accept "finished books;" however, their reviews do not have nearly as much influence on "buys" by libraries, chains and major wholesalers that reviews in the "pre-publication only" organs typically exert.

Royalties—Monies paid by a publisher to an author as a percentage of receipts from sales of a work. Royalties may be based on the retail list price of the work or on net receipts to a publisher (after discounts to distributors and wholesalers). It has become more and more common, over the last twenty years, for publishers to pay royalties "on the net." Fairly common these days are royalties of 5-7 percent on retail list price of a work and 9-12 percent on net receipts. Escalator clauses may raise the royalty percentage for authors after certain sales benchmarks are achieved— for instance, 10 percent royalty on net receipts up to 5,000 copies sold, thence 12.5 percent up to 10,000 copies sold, and 15 percent after 10,000 copies.

Saddlestitched—Double or triple stapling as binding for small books, usually under 80 pages (when book is not thick enough to create a "spine").

Self publishing—Creation of one's own publishing house for the purpose of issuing a book. Self publishing works best when an author can start with a sizable database of potential purchasers of the projected book and has a good handle on how best to market to that prospect pool. When a new self publisher must rely on trade bookstores for the lion's share of sales, he or she is setting up a steep challenge.

Sell sheet—Single-sided sheet containing all publication data on a book plus a blurb, endorsements and a line or two about the author. Sell sheets are presented to buyers at the bookstore chains, to wholesalers and also to independent bookstores to generate orders for new titles—typically several months before the publication date.

Sell through—See p.77 (#86).

Shelving category—See p.49 (#53).

Signature—Group of pages to run on a web press and then be folded and cut to form book pages. Signatures run in eights: 8, 16, 24, 32. Most commonly printers run books in signatures of 16 pages. The number of pages in a book will, thus, almost invariably be a multiple of eight.

Slush pile—Place at a publishing house where unsolicited manuscripts are put. Most publishers eventually have a lower-level employee inspect these submissions; however, many, if not most, are sent back to their writers unread, with a boilerplate rejection note (if return postage has accompanied the submission).

Spine—See p.49 (#54).

Style—Guide for language usage—syntax, grammar, punctuation—that a given publisher follows. The Chicago Manual of Style, published by the University of Chicago Press, has long been considered the main reference source for questions of style in U.S. book publishing. Some of the larger publishing houses, however, have put together their own style manuals, roughly based on "Chicago."

Subsidy press—Not all fee-for-publishing presses operate as vanity presses. Quality subsidy presses will insist on a rigorous editorial and graphic development of a work that has intrinsic merit for circulation. Authors nonetheless pay all editorial, graphic, printing, binding, shipping and warehousing costs in exchange for a much larger share of receipts from sales.

Title page—Either follows the half-title page or opens the book if no half title page is used. Printed here is the book's title, followed by the subtitle, the author's name— often, but not always, centered on the page, followed by the publisher's colophon (see colophon). The author's name should never be in a point size as high as the title. Typically it should be no larger than the subtitle.

Traditional publishing—In this mode, the publisher will contract with an author to publish a work and will agree to bear all costs of book production, sales and distribution. Such a publisher may or may not offer an advance against royalties. All will agree to pay royalties on book sales (See "royalties"). Even in traditional publishing, however, there is usually an implicit or explicit understanding that authors will spend their own time and money on marketing the book. Note: Marketing money frequently exceeds sums spent on typesetting and printing on a given book.

Trim size—Dimensions of a book page after trimming. Some standard trim sizes for books are: 5 x 7, 5 x 8, 5.5 x 8.5, 6 x 9, 6 x 10, 9 x 12. Other trim sizes are possible but may be more expensive if a given printer does not consider that size "standard." In general, too, trade bookstores prefer standard sizes.

Unsolicited ms.—Manuscript sent to a publisher with no verbal or written invitation on the publisher's part to receive it and review it. . . (See slush pile.)

Vanity press—Publisher that will agree, for a fee, to publish a work submitted by an author without regard for the merit of the work or an eye to its marketability. Be aware that a number of nationally prominent vanity publishers have been blacklisted by Barnes & Noble and Borders and also by smaller chains and some major independent bookstores.

MAJOR MEDIA LISTS

The top 10 media markets

New York
Los Angeles
Chicago
Philadelphia
San Francisco
Boston
Dallas
Washington
Atlanta
Detroit

The top 50 newspapers by circulation

Newspaper	Circulation
USA Today	2,246,996
The Wall Street Journal	2,091,062
The New York Times	1,118,565
Los Angeles Times	955,211
The Washington Post	778,416
Daily News	729,124
New York Post	652,426
Chicago Tribune	613,509
Newsday	579,351
Houston Chronicle	553,018
The Dallas Morning News	525,441

San Francisco Chronicle	512,649
Chicago Sun-Times	481,798
Boston Globe	450,538
The Arizona Republic	432,284
The Star-Ledger	408,192
Atlanta Journal-Constitution	382,421
Star Tribune	380,354
Philadelphia Inquirer	376,493
The Plain Dealer	365,288
Detroit Free Press	363,490
Chinese Daily News	359,900
World Journal: New York Edition	359,900
The San Diego Union-Tribune	346,387
The Oregonian	343,661
St. Petersburg Times	314,104
Miami Herald	304,795
The Baltimore Sun	304,244
Sacramento Bee	302,804
Denver Post	301,108
Rocky Mountain News	301,005
The Orange County Register	300,888
St. Louis Post-Dispatch	286,939
San Jose Mercury News	276,787
The Kansas City Star	273,723
The Times-Picayune	260,720
The News Tribune	258,400
Orlando Sentinel	257,429
The Columbus Dispatch	256,547
The Indianapolis Star	255,286

World Journal: Los Angeles Edition	250,000
Investor's Business Daily	248,215
Boston Herald	247,885
Milwaukee Journal Sentinel	244,288
Pittsburgh Post-Gazette	242,546
The Charlotte Observer	242,082
San Antonio Express-News	239,912
Seattle Times	239,470
The Tampa Tribune	238,176
South Florida Sun-Sentinel	234,254

The top wire services

Associated Press
Reuters
United Press International (UPI)
Bloomberg
New York Times Syndicate
Tribune Media Services
King Features
Scripps Howard News Service
Copley News Service
Knight Ridder/Tribune Information Services
Gannett News Service

The top 20 consumer publications by circulation

Publication	Circulation
Reader's Digest	11,000,000
TV Guide	9,061,639
Better Homes & Gardens	7,607,832
National Geographic Magazine	6,685,684
Good Housekeeping	4,690,508
Family Circle	4,601,708
Ladies' Home Journal	4,101,280
Woman's Day	4,065,406
Consumer Reports	4,000,000
Time	4,000,000
People	3,350,000
Prevention	3,150,017
Newsweek	3,125,151
Cosmopolitan	2,860,024
Sports Illustrated	2,700,000
Guideposts Magazine	2,656,662
Southern Living	2,546,471
O, The Oprah Magazine	2,532,621
Maxim	2,512,090
Seventeen	2,431,943

The top 10 business publications by circulation

Publication	Circulation
FSB: Fortune Small Business	1,000,000
BusinessWeek	987,369
Forbes	922,252
Fortune	875,520
Fast Company	734,449
Priority	720,000
Inc	680,719
MyBusiness	554,077
Entrepreneur Magazine	550,000
Black Enterprise Magazine	467,900

The top 10 Internet sites

Internet Site	Visitors Each Month
Yahoo!	45,774,000
msn	44,651,000
CNET News.com	44,400,000
LYCOS	33,364,000
pbs.org	25,241,956
About.com	24,868,000
Netscape Netcenter	23,972,000
AOL.com	23,394,000
BusinessWire.com	22,000,000
MSNBC.com	20,584,000

About the Authors

CELIA ROCKS and **DOTTIE DEHART** spend most of their time publicizing their clients' brilliance. This sales, marketing and public relations firm—which has offices in both Pennsylvania and North Carolina—features three distinct divisions:

* **Rocks-DeHart Public Relations (RDPR)**, the "umbrella" under which the other divisions fall, is devoted to book publicity. The company consists of the best writers, media specialists, publicists, branding strategists and graphic designers—all focused on branding and marketing initiatives. Founded in 1993 by Celia and her business partner, Dottie DeHart, it produces a full range of services. For more information, please visit www.rdpr.com.

* **Brilliance Marketing Management**, a rapidly growing division of RDPR, helps corporations in many industries—as well as individual

executives, speakers and consultants—pinpoint, refine and communicate the strengths that make them unique. The Brilliance team often may be found conducting intensive audit "workdays" in search of a client's brilliance—that innate and unique quality upon which powerful identities are built. The goal of this program is to craft effective, long-term strategies for increasing sales. To learn more about Brilliance Marketing, visit www.brilliancemarketing.com.

* **Brilliance Workshops & Seminars**, another RDPR division, offers intensive company-wide instruction regarding the principles set forth in this book.

Celia lives in Pittsburgh, Pennsylvania, and Dottie lives in Conover, North Carolina. You may contact Celia or Dottie via either the website listed above or call them directly at 412-784-8811.

Celia and Dottie have been written about in national newspapers and magazines such as *Investor's Business Daily*, *Southwest Airlines Magazine*, *Fortune Small Business*, *Working Woman*, *Working Mother*, *Woman's Day* and *Self Magazine*.

Acknowledgments

Our thanks to Patrick Grace, Ph.D., of Grace Associates, for sharing his knowledge and love of publishing with us.

Richard, Frank and Elizabeth, I love you.

- Celia Rocks

To all our clients who have made us better people by sharing their wisdom with us.

To the team of professionals at Rocks-DeHart Public Relations (Celia, Paige, Ashley, Kati, Anna, Charity and Ann). Your talent, creativity and tenacious work ethic make me proud to be associated with you.

- Dottie DeHart